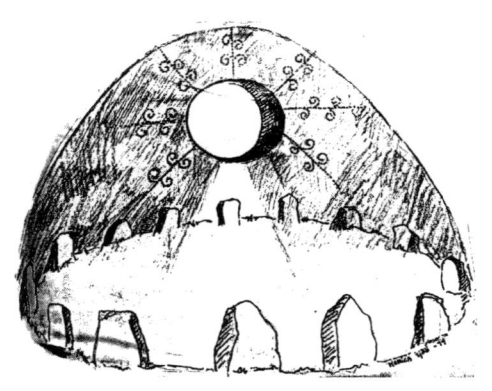

Spiral Journey:

Stages of an initiation into Her Mysteries

Monica Sjöö

Front cover: Sheela-Na-Gig Creation (1978). Back cover: Monica in her garden in Wales with 'Celebrating Ancient Celtic Wales/Cymru' (1983)

ISBN 978-0-9932164-5-9

Copyright © 2018
www.antennapublications.org.uk
www.facebook.com/MonicaSjooLifeandLetters

ANTENNA PUBLICATIONS

Every effort had been made to trace the copyright holders of the photographs in the book, but one or two were unreachable. We would be grateful if the photographers concerned would contact us.

Monica 8/50   Moon/sun/sky & Earth Goddess at Silbury   Equinox 1984

CONTENTS

FOREWORD

During Monica's occasional visits to my home I often felt awestruck, and sometimes overwhelmed by her energy, and by the vast range of her commitments. Little did I realize that in addition to the innumerable social networks to which she contributed, and to her substantial work as an artist and a mother, she was also writing a grand collection of essays, which are now my pleasure to introduce.

In these, as in her other activities, she was able to find and vividly describe the underlying pattern that united her many journeys. Thus in her 'Coming Full Circle' she is able to unify a wide range of eras and places while preserving the particular flavour of each location.

Every reader is bound to react in his or her own way to her achievement, and for me it brings to mind the epitome of the continuously pregnant world personified by Silbury Hill in Wiltshire, surrounded by her Goddess-shaped moat and her natural equivalent at the nearby Swallowhead Spring.

Monica's cyclings, set forth in her essays, by chance correspond to those described by the renowned archaeologist Maria Gimbutas in her 'Language of the Goddess' (1989), and include Death and Regeneration, with renewed energy unfolding again as found in phases of the human, animal and vegetable life-cycles.

The sadness and sense of loss that so many of us feel over Monica's death is slightly mitigated by the realisation that, in dying, she has personally contributed to the completion of the cycle that she did so much to promote during her amazing lifetime.

Considering her typically selfless attitude, she may not mind if I attach this recently rewritten version of the Lord's Prayer in my tribute to her, and to the planet about which she cared so much, and spoke so passionately:

Our Lady's Prayer

Our Mother, who art the Earth, Hallowed be thy World.
Thy will be done, as you plough the rain-soaked furrows, source of our daily bread.
Thanks to your Spirit-within-Matter you also free us from the curse of Original Sin, and our inherited guilt vanishes.
Now the Sacred Apples on your world Paradise tree enable Eternity to appear in every Seasonal Round,
While tiny genes are allowed to transmit life-everlasting,
For ever and ever.
Amen.

Thank you Monica. I'm enjoying the read.

Michael Dames - Samhain 2018

Editors note: Monica Sjöö's first language was Swedish, and her writing in English could be ungrammatical at times. This is somewhat apparent in the appendix, 'Women's Dream-journeying across Salisbury Plain': an important but unedited chapter of 'Spiral Journey' that was added to the manuscript after the main body of the text had been completed. Val Remy, who typed up the rest of the book and acted as the original editor, opted for an unusual use of capital letters, in particular choosing a lower-case when writing eg 'christ', 'christianity' or 'roman catholic'. This convention has been retained.
RW

INTRODUCTION

In 1976 I first attempted writing a long article about the religion of the Cosmic Mother. Later, together with a co-writer, the New Mexico poet Barbara Mor, the original writing was vastly extended and in 1981 was published as a full-length book called *The Ancient Religion of the Great Cosmic Mother of All* by the Rainbow Press in Trondheim, Norway.

Much has happened since that first time when I tried to express my belief in and knowledge of the Goddess in writing in a coherent way. Since 1979 I have made many journeys to the ancient sacred places of the Goddess, in the Celtic world, in other parts of Europe and on Crete, and I have been deeply influenced and changed by Her powers that still reside in the Earth, the Wells, Mountains and Standing Stones of these sacred sites and ritual centres.

Being primarily a visual artist these experiences have deeply affected my paintings and have inspired the exhibition *Woman-Magic, Celebrating the Goddess Within Us* that has travelled during the last few years both in England and Northern Europe and Scandinavia.

I feel that our book on the Cosmic Mother is a sort of Herstory, an attempt at understanding the inner meaning of the religion of the Goddess for ancient women and men, and also for us today. I have recently felt an increasing need to complement this by writing a personal account, a tale weaving together the threads of my own experiences and pilgrimages, following the Earth Spirit on Her paths over a number of years and thereby also telling the background story of where my paintings come from and what inspires them.

This time I do not have a co-writer, but a very good friend, Valerie Remy, who has gone through my manuscript word for word and edited with me. She also took on the daunting task of typing it all out. I am grateful to her for her help and support. Also without Keith Motherson's help and love and support in looking after this mother's son some of my journeys would not have been possible.

Val was with me on that miraculous day when we discovered together the Bleeding Yew Mother in Nevern graveyard here in Pembrokeshire. For this story and many others you will have to begin the Spiral Journey... I hope that you will enjoy it.

Blessed Be in the Goddess,

Monica Sjöö

Dyfed, Wales, Full Moon 17/3/84.

AUTOBIOGRAPHICAL NOTE

I was born in the north of Sweden in 1938 (the year that the atom was split), but have lived most of my adult life in Bristol, England, and for the last four years in Pembrokeshire in Cymru/Wales. Between 1965-67 I lived in Stockholm for a period where I worked with the anti-imperialist movement, particularly against the Vietnam War, and organised several Vietnam art exhibitions.

Since the beginning of the present Women's Liberation Movement in 1969 I have been active in grassroots campaigns such as the Women's Abortion and Contraception Campaign (WACC), Wages for Housework, the Bristol Gay Women's Group and the Claimants Union in which I worked with unsupported mothers.

For the last few years I have been mainly involved in exhibiting and working with Feminist artists both in Britain and abroad, with the Matriarchy Network, the Women for Life on Earth network, radical Pagans, and Fishguard CND.

As well as painting I have also written a great deal, and in 1979 produced and published a joint pamphlet with Keith Motherson called *Women are the Real Left/Wider We: Towards an Anarchist Politics* (Matri-anarchy Publications) which included articles which we had each written over a period of many years, a number of which had been published in Peace News.

I have also written many articles on Feminist art and on the religion of the Goddess. In 1981 my full-length book (co-written with New Mexico poet Barbara Mor), *The Ancient Religion of the Great Cosmic Mother of All* was published by the Rainbow Press in Norway.

Since 1967 I have had many exhibitions, mostly collectively with other women artists both in Britain and Sweden. Since December 1979 we have had a collective exhibition on the road called *Woman-Magic: Celebrating the Goddess Within Us*. Originally the contributors were Marika Tell (who is also Swedish), with her batiks and ceramic pots, Beverly Skinner (an American painter who has, like me, lived half a lifetime in

Bristol), and myself. After travelling around England for two years the exhibition has, since September 1982, been shown in Denmark, Germany and Sweden. The contributors are now, besides myself and Beverly Skinner, the Birmingham artist Anne Berg and Lynne Wood from Australia. Our images are of the Goddess and Earth Magic.

The inspiration for my paintings over the years has been my woman-experiences of natural childbirth (I have three children), bisexuality, menstrual creative and psychic powers, visions and dreams of the Goddess and of ancient women, the herstory (not history) of women of all cultures and 'races', and journeys to Her sacred sites.

For me there has never been any contradiction between working politically with women at the same time as trying to understand and tune into our spirituality, the Goddess within us. That Feminist art is, in itself, highly political I have learned from bitter experience. In 1968 I did the large (six feet high) painting God Giving Birth, showing my religious conception of the Cosmic creative power as the Mother of All. She is a woman of indistinct 'race' (not white) standing in space while giving birth. This image nearly landed me in court for 'obscenity and blasphemy' in St. Ives, Cornwall, in 1970, in London in 1973 and in Lancaster in 1980. Attempts are being made to censure my painting and prosecute me: this in a society where the most violent and obscene pornography, which always degrades, humiliates and does violence to women, is acceptable and allowed. These images that dehumanize women are everywhere - in advertising, films, videos and the press. What apparently is not permitted are images like ours that empower women and show us as powerful, creative and at the same time sexual subjects. Women are sick to the teeth with this situation.

Unless women, together with oppressed people everywhere, rise up, unless we again heal ourselves and this sacred Earth that has been plundered, ravaged and raped at the instigation of ruling and predatory men in patriarchal capitalist societies, unless we can again live in harmony with Her, we will all die. The Mother is calling us at this late hour. She is rising within us. She is empowering the women at Greenham Common who are an example to women everywhere - and also to many men. She is speaking through the Native Americans, the Samis of the North, the Aborigines of Australia, and we must heed their warning when they tell us that our Mother, the Earth, is suffering, that She will tolerate no more abuse to Her living body, no more uranium mining, no more acid rain, no more cutting down of Her forests, no more poisoning of Her seas. We must live in harmony with all Her living plants, animals and creatures or we have no right to live at all: we will have overstayed our welcome on this Earth.

Living in the countryside here in Pembrokeshire has brought me infinitely closer to an understanding of Her seasons, of growth and decay, death and rebirth in Nature. We have so much to re-learn about the natural, healing powers of the Earth and Her waters. We must tune back into the darkness of the night-time and Her Lunar powers of imagination, visions and dreams, into Her dark cosmic body. Matter-Mater-Mother is alive and enspirited and there are no divisions (only 'manmade' ones) between body and soul, matter and spirit. We must be graceful enough to return love and care to our Mother who gave us life.

Overleaf: Meeting the Ancestors at Avebury (1993)

INITIATION AT AVEBURY/SILBURY

My life and painting changed greatly after an experience I had of the Mother Goddess at Avebury/Silbury in 1978. Although my telling of this experience has already been published in other places[1] I still want it included here in its true context:

"Five days after Imbolc/Bride's Day, the ancient quarter-day Fire Festival of the pre-Celtic Brigid who was worshipped by the Celts until very recently. Imbolc means 'ewe's milk' and was celebrated by the Celts as the first day of Spring when the penned-up animals were let out in the fields and the first lambs were born. Brigia/Bride was the Goddess of healing, of the flocks and of plantlife, of childbirth, the waters, fire, smithcraft and poetry. Perhaps anciently Avebury/Silbury was Hers...or belonged to Anu/Danu. Danu/Bride was probably the original mother/daughter unity. They were the same as Demeter/Kore of the ancients and of the Celts of these isles.

We arrived on a beautiful late winter's day at Avebury village, parked the old post office van and ate our mushroom salad. The village is built within the stone circle, is contained within it. (The Neolithic stone circle at Avebury is the largest one in Northern Europe.) ... Amazing, rough, squat, colossal stones...seeming like human bodies and gigantic heads. Here one feels is THE centre of the Mother Goddess. What would it be like living in this village, being part of Her living body? The earth around the stone circle is shaped and moulded in ridges and ditches. Many of the stones are mutilated, like half a head chopped off...painful to see. Many are missing, and ugly looking triangular-shaped stones have been positioned to mark where they fell or once stood. They look like the gravestones they really are. During the Witch-Hunts/Burning Times the stones were deliberately destroyed, split apart and buried. The church feared their power. There still remains a great power, beauty and mystery in this whole space and its stones.

We follow the earth-works around the entire circle and then slowly follow the remains of West Kennet stone avenue as it winds its way across the fields.

The magic mushrooms (in the salad we had mixed in some psilocybin) have now taken effect... I long and long to arrive at Silbury Mound, the pregnant Earth Womb of the Mother. We have seen her in the distance from the road and from the village. I clutch a stone in my hand for safety and we plod across the ploughed and muddy fields, having eternally to cross barbed-wire fences. Gripped by panic, unable to either remain or to cross over the ugly, now seeming just so offensive, fences; wanting to find comfort and refuge with the

18

A sea Earth works dream.

Breast/Eye/Womb-belly rising out of the landscape so naked and so vulnerable, we scramble through what seems like marshland and wilderness. I feel as if transported thousands of years back in time. We come closer to Her womb and discover that on the road by Her side there is parked a square bright red lorry with the name 'Peter Lord' written on its side... LORD...oh no...is there nowhere, not even in Her presence when one is allowed to forget about patriarchy and its deadly godhead?

Nearer Her Mound we discover notices that say 'The monument is closed due to erosion'. Her Womb, surrounded by water, is everywhere shut off by treble layers of barbed-wire fences. Feeling stunned...the earth around the mound appears to move and flicker... some swans are frozen motionless... I feel caught in eternity. Some teenagers scramble past us up the mound. We follow them, hoping that they won't talk with us, we who are from another century. Feeling of fear at caring to trample on Her belly, the grass matted and unkempt. A man shouts from the road: 'Get down from there!' We sit down on the side of the Mound furthest away from the road; the teenagers disappear out of sight and hearing. I am overtaken with a sudden and enormous grief... the Mother...the entire Mound cries through me. I am at one with Her, grieving at our lost women-cultures...the pollution and death of her land all around us.

What have they done to you, Mother, what have they done...what have they done...? Man shouts from the road. I feel overwhelming fear...am a hunted female animal...got to flee...got to get down from Her womb and away from the road, away. The road appears to stand for everything alien and evil: motors, men with patriarchal authority, oppression. Shots are heard regularly in the distance. (Wiltshire Plain, where Avebury is situated, and Salisbury Plain, where Stonehenge stands, are used for army exercises and are military bases.) ...aeroplanes continuously overhead...evil, evil, danger...

Almost run, slide down her side...walk slowly...great effort, fear... tracing our way around the water-moat, back into the fields from where we came. Feeling of victory; we had avoided the road...we are safe...we are still within Her Nature. I look at Her Mound...so exposed... like veins on a breast streaking Her sides...again overwhelmed by tears and sorrow. I now understand what Mother Earth means...something so enormous, powerful...also so painful in my own woman's body which is like Hers...violent but gentle... powerful but vulnerable.

Slowly we follow the river, feeling myself floating with her... flowing with the wonderful water formations...dancing along with Her serpentine rhythms. Sudden sharp halt at the sight of the pollution of the waters and the rubbish accumulated there...anger, anger. More barbed-wire fences... We follow the direction leading to West Kennet Long Barrow and walk up a long mud track. We see the long Barrow at the summit and the enormous stones covering the entrance. We walk around the stones... and SUDDENLY...we see the stark blackness from the entrance of the cunt/mouth into her underground womb. Fear at being swallowed up by the so intense darkness...but I overcome the fear and enter... totally another world is there... of mystery...of power...of peace. Sounds are amplified in here and the stone chambers appear for a timeless moment to breathe. I feel like gyrating...I feel like a Spiral...then feel a great urge to sleep on the floor in the uterus-room at the end of the passage ...great stillness in Her living darkness. Feeling infinitely 'higher' within the tomb/temple than when re-entering the world outside... strange and powerful vibrations (perhaps emanating from powerful underground waters?)... here no feeling of sorrow and vulnerability. This is the place of the Winter/Death/ Cosmic Waters/Rebirth/the Dark aspect of the Goddess...we are here within Her season and we are welcome...

We walk down the mud track...feeling an enormous tiredness and exhaustion... just want to sleep...to sleep. We trace our way back to Avebury village across the fields and the public footpaths...we retrace our way around the stone circle and arrive six hours later back at our van and drive off..."

I wrote the above in February 1978 and am now writing this *Spiral Journey* in February 1983, in the season of Bride. During the five years that have gone by since this original initiation into Her mysteries I have visited Avebury/Silbury many times at different seasons and various times of day and night. A particularly moving occasion was when some friends of mine involved in the British Pagan/Feminist/Goddess newsletter 'Wood and Water' celebrated the birth of their first-born child by having a 'birthing ceremony' within West Kennet Long Barrow. We all witnessed how Hilary said to her child "Here child, know thy Mother", and to the Goddess, "Here Mother, receive thy child", as we gathered within the darkness of Her Womb. I feel that it is so very important for our sanity that we recreate and re-enact the Mysteries of return into Her Womb - in caves, underground chambers, dark space - to gain illumination, visions and dreams; to be reborn, to return into the Lunar consciousness which in all patriarchies is so denied, slandered and feared.

Until very recently Avebury/Silbury were not popularly known, while Stonehenge, a far more patriarchal and solar-oriented temple, has been known far and wide. It was only with the publication of Michael Dames' wonderful books 'Silbury Treasure, the Great Goddess Rediscovered' (1977) and 'The Avebury Cycle' (1978) that many women, myself included, began to understand that this is the very ancient sacred centre and Body of the Neolithic Mother[2]. It is significant that in the National Trust bookshop in Avebury itself they will not sell Michael Dames' books and that the people who live there insist on seeing Silbury Mound as the grave of some Bronze Age male chieftain. The reason the mound is eroding is because archaeologists have spent the last 200 years digging (or should we call it raping?) it, desperately trying to find a non-existent grave! Michael Dames' books have been ridiculed by the entire male academic community and also by the self-styled gurus of the New Age scene, patriarchs who will not admit that the Neolithic culture of the sacred stones was created by women, that women were both the ancient farmers and shaman/astronomers.

West Kennet Long Barrow: Abode of the Light/Dark Mother (1989)

The first time I had experienced the Goddess - had sensed Her powers within me - had been at the natural home birth of my second child, now 21 years ago. From then on I had felt that I was mystically in communication with, and guided in my painting by ancient women who perhaps in fact co-exist with us still, in a different dimension of reality.

I feel as if I receive the images in my paintings from ancient times... as though I am but a medium for an energy wanting to be expressed and given form. I feel that the British Isles were probably sacred islands of the North, as Malta and Crete were in the South. Everywhere on these islands one comes across remains of ancient cultures and there is still great power that we can reach and be transformed by, embedded within the stones, the earth and the waters, in the sacred places. If one is present there - with the true openness and reverence - at certain times of the year when the Spirit roams through the land and the Moon is in Her appropriate phase, then one is profoundly changed in one's psyche and awareness. This is as true today as it was in the past.

It has been said that there is a strange light and colour scale in my paintings, as if they are imbued with moonlight. This is probably also a quality of the snow that I experienced in the north of Sweden in the winters as a child; the Moon reflected in snow crystals emanating a wonderful eerie and mysterious light.

It is strange that during the 'trip' I had at Avebury I should have seen three swans in the watermoat around Silbury Mound, since these are sacred birds of the Goddess. There are many tales of Fairy-women transforming themselves into swans. The swans are as white as the snow, the sea foam and the moonlight; and they are powerful and fierce.

At Avebury I was helped by the sacred mushroom psilocybin to enter into Her reality, into another space and time. I feel that these tiny breast-shaped mushrooms - that grow so abundantly all over these islands - are also the Mother's gift to us and one of the many ways in which she is now fighting for Her survival against the matricide (Mother-murder) planned by the nuclear scientists. They even have a tiny nipple and feel benevolent and maternal. They have a way of reaching into the most hidden depths of our psyches and are capable of opening us up to intense communication with living and enspirited Nature all around us. This experience of intense openness to all of organic and growing Nature, feeling its breath and vibrating life, stayed with me for a long time. As a result the sea, stones, mountains and wells have appeared more and more in my images since then. Until that time my work had been mainly concerned with creating large figurative paintings envisioning and bringing the Goddess into being, in powerful women-figures. I was still living in Bristol in the south-west of England, but have since then - for the last three years - lived in Celtic Cymru/Wales.

CELTIC CORNWALL

The experience at Avebury inspired me to seek out Her many sacred places in Britain, and soon, in 1978, I set off with some friends and children in the same old post office van to travel down through Somerset and Devon to ancient and Celtic Kernow/Cornwall. We went through Dartmoor and Bodmin Moor and were amazed at the wealth of ancient remains everywhere around us: Neolithic stone circles and cromlechs, standing stones and cairns, Bronze Age hut circles and Iron Age forts, in areas now totally uninhabited and desolate.

We visited a magnificent dolmen/cromlech ('Cromlechau' means 'burial chamber' in Welsh) called Spinster's Rock. It stands in a field on Dartmoor. Cromlechs consist of a number of vertical stones surmounted by a giant capstone. Some would have originally been covered with a mound of earth and stone; others would never have been burial places, but places of power to do with the underground waters.

It is said of this cromlech that it was built by a giant woman, or Cailleach (the Hag, Crone or Wise Woman) who moves mountains and carries the massive stones of the sacred circles and cairns in Her apron. There are myths about Her in Ireland and Scotland. Obviously She was originally Danu, Goddess of the stone/Megalith builders; She was the tomb-Goddess of Death and Rebirth[3]. Some of the cromlechs were both places of collective burial (like the early christian churches), as well as places of worship, high energies and mysterious powers. There are innumerable remains of fires and feasting in and by the barrows.

There were no individual burials until the Bronze Age with its hierarchical and warlike society, introduced in Britain by the Beaker People from ca. 2000 b.c. The Mother Goddess was the guardian of the seed hidden in the Earth: She was the guardian of the Dead awaiting rebirth, like the seed, through Her. The newly Dead were seen to be particularly powerful and could be contacted during shamanistic trances within the darkness of the vulva-shaped Cromlech, when important healing and prophetic knowledge could be gained through them. The Dead were thought to await rebirth inside the Earth Womb, on the

Moon or the Milky Way. The cromlechs and barrows symbolised the entrance - the Womb of Death and Rebirth - to the ancestral spirit-world, the Otherworld, the Dream-Place of past and present, where psychic and physical realities merge. The ancient communal tomb was the source of power where energies meet and where one is closer to the sacred. Women and men shamans in all ages have retreated into caves and rock-cut chambers to gain knowledge and to communicate with the spirit-world of the Goddess. This was so on Crete and is still so among many natural peoples.

Men-an-Tol and Avebury (1978)

The Megalithic stone monuments and the Neolithic culture of Britain and Ireland, like that in Brittany, were created by an ancient Iberian pre-Celtic people who were small, fine-featured and dark skinned. It is thought that they might have been related to the present-day Samis and Finns of the Far North. Their descendants still live on the fringes of the Celtic world. Their Shamans would have been women who guarded the

Mysteries and led the rituals, communicating with the Dead and the Otherworld. The ancient Britons were peaceful, understood the calendar, knew the Solstices and the Lunar alignments. They also believed in reincarnation. The stone circles have been called Lunar temples/observatories. Their most important astrological function was to predict Lunar eclipses and the tides of the seas. A Thom[4] a British civil engineer who measured hundreds of megalithic sites, believes that all the impressive alignments in Britain were Lunar. He also discovered that the ancients used a mathematical measurement which he calls a 'megalithic yard' (2.72 feet) and which is based on the length of the human stride. It seems that ancient women used a kind of holistic mathematics that has been lost to us today and had great knowledge of the movements of the planets, the Moon and the Sun; knowledge we have yet to recover. Lunar also means menstrual, which is obvious to any woman. The Stones were a kind of menstrual calendar set up in the landscape within which were performed rituals in the moonlight. The menhirs had oracular functions and were called 'speaking stones'.

Orgiastic rites would have been held in the light of the Full Moon as well, for the Full Moon is the giver of all creativity and fertility of mind, psyche and body. Any children born as a result of heterosexual rites would have been called 'Virgin-born', mothered by the Moon. There appears to be a link between women's sexuality and religious experience. Women are capable of integrating sexual pleasure into the high brain centre and can, through sexual experience, reach transcendental heights and altered states of being. This doesn't appear to be true for the human male. Also, unlike most female mammals, women are not bound by ovarian cycles. The function of our sexuality is therefore NOT purely reproductive.

In the Goddess-religions ecstatic sexual rites expressing all forms of sexuality are integral to Her worship, while male-centred 'religions' practise denial of sexuality (particularly in women) and attempt to separate mind from body, spirit from matter, and enforce rigid male-controlled heterosexuality. Patriarchy replaces eroticism and freely given orgiastic sexuality with rape, pornography and monogamous 'wifehood' imposed on women. In the Goddess-cultures men were, so far as they were allowed to be initiated at all, initiated into the Mysteries by women. This is still so in Tantra, and was so among the Celts.

The stones and the Stone Circles are always associated with the Waters. They are encircled by underground waters and are placed above geodetic Spirals of great magic and healing powers. They are placed by wells and rivers, by the sea or on sacred islands surrounded by water on all sides. The great oceans are the Mother of all life and the wells springing up from inside of the Earth were felt to be her menstrual/lifegiving and healing blood. The stone circles are never exact geometric circles, but are organic and resemble wombs, caves and pots.

There are many stone circles near Land's End in Kernow/Cornwall and some of them are called 'Merry Maidens', 'Nine Maidens' and so on. The story goes that the Stones had once been foolish young women who had been dancing and merry-making on the sabbath and therefore were petrified as a punishment by the vengeful, puritanical and joyless Jehovah. The 'Pipers' who accompanied the dance, are some large stones standing near the circles. This story is told of many circles. 'Dans Meyn' means Dancing Stones in Cornish. Interestingly enough the local people associate the Stone Circles with women, dancing and music - and defiance of the patriarchal male god!

There are scientists and 'ley line' enthusiasts (ley lines are the energy lines thought to connect the stones and sacred places along certain paths that are also known as 'Fairy paths') who have spent some years now investigating the energies given off by the Stones of the Rollright Circle in England. They call their research 'The Dragon Project'. The Dragon/Serpent represents the geodetic Spiral patterns of the serpentine underground waters and the magnetic current of the Earth Spirit. The Goddess as Dragon/Serpent is the chthonic powers of the Earth and Waters, while in bird form, she is Air and sky.

One thing there seems to be agreement about is that there is an extraordinary amount of quartz in the Sacred Stones everywhere. Quartz is a crystalline mineral and a carrier of electro-magnetic currents. It is thought to have healing powers and to dispense wisdom and the power of divination (fortune-tellers use a crystal ball of quartz) and it was (and still is) universally used in shamanistic rituals. Near where I live in Wales there is a magnificent cromlech situated on the very beautiful coast with the sea behind it. Half of its upright stones are just plain grey granite, while their opposite numbers, facing them, are stones speckled with large chunks of quartz. The enormous capstone, weighing 25 tons, has a similar quartz content. This stone was obviously chosen for a reason.

26

It has also been found that certain standing stones associated with stone circles generate ultrasound when stimulated by elements in the electromagnetic spectrum radiated by the Sun at dawn. Many musical instruments and women's singing contain ultrasound which is a sound or a frequency too high for the human ear to detect. Someone writing in the English journal, "The Ley Hunter: Magazine for Earth Mysteries", put forward the following theory a few years ago. If a specific number of young girls with high piping voices danced within a circle of standing stones they would subject each stone to a burst of sound energy as each girl passed it. The ultrasound in the voices would act on the crystal structure of the stone causing the electromagnetic radiation to be a fixed frequency dependent upon the physical characteristics of the quartz content. It seems possible that with certain numbers of dancers singing and humming a special note, a type of resonance might be set up in the circle, the radiation from each stone arriving at its neighbour at the right time to reinforce the effect of each girl's voice as she passed each stone. A fully energised circle at the climax of a nine-maiden power ritual would have a pulse of vibrating energy swirling around the circle. We don't know whether or not this energy was then aimed at triggering off outlying stones (as some kind of 'church bells') to be carried throughout the land, acting on the fertility of the plant world and on the psychic telepathic powers of the human communities. *Like a singing bowl,*

It is interesting to see that within the Craft, in the covens, the participants also dance within a circle so as to build up a psychic power cone which can then be directed towards a certain goal - to heal or to destroy. It has been suggested that the ancient 'straight line' grid system of the 'leys' was in fact already an early attempt at containment of female creative energies and a scheme towards control, centralisation and kingship. The Earth Spirit doesn't move in a straight line but in constantly flowing serpentine and spiral movements. One hears again and again in early patriarchal accounts how the head of the Serpent was staked by driving pegs into the ground and held static, presumably by the emerging male priesthood which was attempting to take over and coopt the powers of the women Shamans. And how the Dragon/Monster was slaughtered by the masculine hero. Out of the dead body of the Mother he then fashions the male universe and creates 'law and order'.

It is interesting that it is mainly men involved in the present-day ley line research. The name of their journal 'The Ley Hunter' gives me a vision of men with guns stalking the Earth's energies. Surely 'The Ley Seeker' would have been a more appropriate and respectful name.

The magnetic Dragon-energies of the Stones/Earth/Minerals/ Underground Waters have to be approached with the greatest respect. We don't know what energies we might naively and wrongfully tamper with. It might also be that unless we regain the knowledge of how to yet again tune into and help reactivate these energies of the Moon, Waters, Earth, Stones and Wells within and without ourselves, we will all die...

I feel that the ancient women knew how to be at one with, and how to affect the radiant energies of the Cosmic Dance and that to them matter and spirit were One and undivided. And it seems to me that present-day male atomic scientists are involved in the exact reversal of the life-affirming process. Instead of tuning into the Cosmic Dance they are aspiring to universal death through the unleashing of deadly energies, such as radiation from the breakdown of the very structures of matter. Barrenness is a patriarchal condition, and vengeance, death, divisiveness and sterility are the names of its male godhead. Scientists want to destroy all of life, reversing millions of years of evolution, as well as wanting to be able to create life artificially by cloning and test-tube babies without the 'aid' of women.

The Cornish stone circles often consist of nineteen not very large stones, a number important in fertility ritual and Lunar calculations. The Megalithic peoples and the Druids after them used a 19-19-18 year eclipse cycle for Lunar calculations. Holed stones were widely believed to possess healing powers. We visited one such stone, called 'Men-an-Tol' or 'Crick stone', on a bleak moor near Morvah. It was believed to have a Fairy guardian who could work miraculous cures. Children who were suffering from rickets were passed through its hole nine times and barren women who did so were thought to become fertile. Holed stones were positioned universally at the entrance of burial chambers and symbolised the birth passage of the Mother in rites of initiation and rebirth. We crawled through the 'Crick stone' in the constant mud and rain. We spent the best part of a month travelling up and down Cornwall seeking out stone circles in farmers' fields, on moorland, in valleys and on mountainsides, most of the time in the pouring rain!

I had already lived a winter by the sea in St. Ives in Cornwall in 1958 and had experienced its wildness and beauty. Many artists, like Barbara Hepworth, have lived there and have been inspired by the strange cliff

28

and rock formations, the luminous almost Mediterranean light, the desolate moorlands and the rugged coastline. In fact Barbara Hepworth became world-famous precisely because of her 'holed stones', sculptures directly inspired by the pebbles and rocks of the area.

NEW GRANGE, HER ANCIENT TEMPLE IN IRELAND

Soon after this Cornish journey I was able to travel to Eire/Southern Ireland with two of my sons and Marika Tell, a sister Swedish artist. We just so happened to arrive in Dublin in time to take part in the first ever Irish Lesbian conference. Many such 'coincidences' happen when you are seeking Her and the way you travel is as important as it is to reach your goal. I feel that every journey to Her sacred places is like entering a labyrinth, every stage is significant and decides what you will experience when you reach Her still centre. There are no short cuts and everything must be lived through to the full.

In Dublin we met up with Maggie Lannin, an artist and Goddess-daughter, whom I had already known for some years. Together we did a workshop on 'Womanspirituality' at the conference. I also did a slide showing of my work. She took us to the Boyne Valley, about 30 miles north of Dublin in County Meath, to visit the Goddess Neolithic temple/womb/tombs of New Grange, Knowth and Dowth. Thanks to Maggie, who is very familiar with these wonderful dwellings of the Mother, and who knew the women-guides there, we were able to spend some time alone within New Grange without the eternal coach-loads of tourists one normally has to suffer there.

Here within New Grange I felt, as I had done at Avebury/Silbury, a sense of recognition...of coming home...as if here is where I had once belonged. As an artist and a woman, I seemed to recognise a perception of space and form that I felt sure had originated with ancient women... based on their female vision, power and wholeness, and coming from a time when Motherhood was associated with creativity and high energies, but also with meditating stillness...from a time when the Goddess expressed gynandrous energies... yin and yang within Her. Here one senses woman-energies that patriarchal language simply has no expression for. I sensed within New Grange - in Her living Darkness - a maternal power, rounded in enormous stone spaces, that is both healing and fearful, dynamic and at rest. She is beyond all polarities... from Her emanate all energies.

It might be that I personally respond so powerfully to New Grange and to West Kennet Long Barrow, where I had also felt a heightened psychic presence, because I myself was born on New Year's Eve and these temple/barrows are the abode of the Life-in-Death Winter Goddess. And, by the way, the mineral quartz often found in the stones is my Capricornian birth sign stone.

New Grange has in common with Avebury/Silbury and other sacred Goddess centres a human-made earth-mound that was probably originally covered in layers of organic material and faced with quartz, a ditch, ceremonial causeways, numerous small burial sounds, a sacred well, and a large henge of rough-hewn stones and single monoliths. This is equally true of Stonehenge. New Grange measures 700 feet in circumference and about 40-50 feet in height. The earth-mound is now again covered in quartz, which suggests the surface of a large egg which conceals the womb-like cave within. It also gives off a silvery Lunar light. The American writer, Martin Brennan, has written a book called 'The Boyne Valley Vision'[5] which is very interesting but also very infuriating because it is written with such a patriarchal bias, and like all such books it is full of contradictions. Brennan says that New Grange, Knowth and Dowth, are part of a scheme which involves the science, calendar, art and ritual of the Megalithic peoples, and that taken together they represent the whole of the Cosmos. He says quite rightly that New Grange is the Cosmic Egg, symbol of birth and creation, of pure creative female energies. Its centre is the point of origin and the point of return: it is creation within the labyrinth of caves and represents the Spiral Journey of the soul through Death to finding rest and rebirth in the central chamber.

According to Brennan New Grange is the creative aspect of the trinity, Knowth representing balance and union, and Dowth (which means 'Darkness') annihilation and dissipation - "the active power of time which ultimately extinguishes all life". All the monuments relate to the River Boyne in the same way as Avebury/Silbury do to the River Kennet. They both derive much of their power from the sacred waters and the holy healing wells. The temples in the Boyne Valley were probably built around 5,000 years ago and are contemporary with the gigantic healing and oracular Goddess-temples on Malta. Both the Maltese and Boyne Valley temples are carbon dated at ca. 3,300 b.c. The former were built in the shape of a gigantic Mother and extend both underground and above the ground. They were said to have been built in a single night by a woman giant with a baby at Her breast.

New Grange is aligned with the Winter Solstice. At dawn on the 21st of December the Sun's dying ray enters the corbelled opening above the entrance to the mound and travels 66 feet through its stone-built passage and shines against the stone deepest within the womb-chamber. Here all could witness the death and new birth of the Winter Sun from the Mother. This is also the longest moonlit night of the year. Every nineteen years the moonbeam travels the same path and it is probable that this was the mound's most important function to the Neolithic peoples. At Knowth also the Lunar beam enters every nineteenth year, and Brennan says that this creates "the most splendid astronomical phenomenon of the Boyne Valley culture". As we saw this is the number of years of the Lunar eclipse cycle and to the ancients such events were of the greatest and most magical importance. The true significance of this has yet to be rediscovered.

Everywhere within New Grange, in its chambers, on the stones at its entrance, on its walls, there are engraved the symbols for rain and water (zigzags and wavy lines), as well as powerful and beautiful double- and triple Spirals. This sacred form-language New Grange also has in common with the temples on Malta, with the passage tomb on Gavr'inis (Goat Island) on the coast of Brittany too. The Spirals, along with the Serpent and the Labyrinth, symbolise Lunar changes and movement, the risings and settings of the eternal Lunar Mother. Brennan thinks that the signs carved on the gigantic entrance stones are charts that diagrammatically record the movements of celestial spheres (a kind of 'cosmic clock') that the ancients used and knew of, a holistic mathematics that was simultaneously both organic and rational. The large stone basins within the triple chambers were used to produce steam and vapour baths so that the people gathered within the mound to witness the birth of the Sun or the Lunar beam at the Winter Solstice would have entered into trance states and were able to undertake the journeys to the Otherworlds. The ancients knew that at the solstices, equinoxes and eclipses there is a greater natural psychic access to other realities. The Moon and the Sun reflected in the water of the basins and thrown as shadows by the stones might also have been used for astronomical observations.

Near the Boyne Valley temples are the Loughcrew Mountains, and on one side of their crests is the site of a passage grave with stones carved with the Goddess's Spiral eyes. One of the mountains is called 'Sliabh na Caillighe', Mountain of the Sorceress, and one of the cairns there is known as the Witch's Seat. Of the sorceress it was said:

> The sorceress determined now Her tomb to build
> Her ample skirts with stones She filled
> and dropped a heap on Carnmore
> then stepped one thousand yards to Loar,
> and dropped another goodly heap;
> and then with one prodigious leap
> gained Carnberg; and on its height
> displayed the wonders of Her might.

The poem seems to imply that the Cailleach built the Boyne Valley monuments! Katherine Briggs, in 'A Dictionary of Fairies' [7], says that Cailleach Bheur of the Scottish Highlands was the blue-faced lean Hag who personified winter, that She probably was the Great Goddess Danu/Anu of the Britons before the Celts. She has many names all over the Isles, including 'Black Annis', which indicates an ancient origin and a widespread cult resembling that of ancient Diana. Notice here the similarity to the Indian Goddess Kali; like Her the Cailleach is black and blue, which are the colours of the sky and of the Waters of the Deep. She is called the Daughter of Grainne, the Winter Sun, and Solar Mother. She was born each Samhain (October 31st) and went about smiting the earth with blight and calling down the snow. A touch of Her staff brings leaves from the trees; She is the season incarnate. She is the guardian of the animals and has been called 'a Scottish Artemis'. She is the Lady of the Beasts. On May Eve (Beltane) Her reign ends and She throws Her staff beneath a holly bush or gorse and turns into a standing stone until next Samhain. The standing stones are sacred to her. But it was also said that at Beltane She turned into a beautiful maid, that She was really both Goddess of winter and summer, Danu/Cailleach and Brigid/Bride, Mother and Daughter, as one and undivided. Remember all the sagas about the ugly old hag who turns into a beautiful young woman when loved by a man who cares truly for Her in spite of Her appearance. She was also the Guardian of Wells and Streams.

Corn-mother at New Grange

The Cailleach of north-west Scotland captured the Maiden/Bride - who is Her own other self - and holds her prisoner in the vastness of Ben Nevis mountain. On the 1st of February, Bride's Day/Bridget's Day, also known as Imbolc, She re-emerges a beautiful young Maiden. Imbolc was the day when the Celts arranged trial marriages lasting for a year. As the Dark Mother of the Deep Waters, the Cailleach was worshipped in caves with wells and within the barrows of the Dead. Her priestesses were old women. Perhaps it was to honour Her that the Picts, the ancient people of the Highlands, went into battle in the nude, their bodies covered in blue earth paint. They believed that she would make them invulnerable and immortal.

Her real identity has been forgotten and 'Annis' has right from the beginning of patriarchy been used as a bugaboo to frighten children. She is said to be monstrous and dwells in lonely caves on bleak hillsides. There are monumental tombs sacred to Her even on the tops of the 300 foot Mountains of Wicklow. She roams the high Scottish mountains at night, moaning and wailing, and any lonely man who should happen to find himself there becomes Her prey.

Janet McCrickard[8] says that the root syllable AN means 'Heaven' and 'Light', and that Goddesses like Athena, Anahita, Anat, Neith, Nut, Annis and Anna are all connected also with the Great Waters and with the Dark aspect of the Goddess. The Great Waters Goddess was both celestial, being the Rain and Waters of Chaos, and chthonic, dwelling under the Earth and manifesting Herself in the form of Springs, Wells, and the magnetic underwater Dragon Currents. She is both Lunar and Solar. The mind and mental powers are a gift of the Lunar Mother and the fiery energies within us are a gift of the Solar Mother. According to Janet, in ancient Ireland the sun was known as the Goddess Grainne or Granya, and one derivation of New Grange is 'the Cave of Granya'. The temple was later thought to belong to the Celtic father god Dagda, the fairy palace 'Brug na Boinne' of the Queen Goddess Boann and her king Dagda, god of the Earth. Janet thinks that it is probable that New Grange was taken over by a succession of patriarchal cults even before the Celtic Age proper. The entry of the sun into the inner chamber at the Winter Solstice is an enactment of the descent of the Sun Goddess into the central cave, the womb of the Earth, to give parthenogenic birth to Her Daughter self. Because of Martin Brennan's thoroughly and boringly sexist bias he is unable to see the cosmic, creative and universal significance of the religion of the Goddess and he therefore assumes that the solar beam entering the Earth Womb symbolises some kind of sex act between an active solar father and a passive Earth Mother. As Janet points out the 'wives' and 'daughters' of assorted sky gods "are invariably the celestial Goddess demoted, dethroned, tamed, married ore and reduced to servitude" and the cults of the male sun god are often violent and intensely woman-suppressing. They are of a later era and have nothing to do with the Neolithic age of the builders of New Grange.

New Grange, Knowth and Dowth must have been places of the Mysteries comparable to those of the ancient Greek Eleusis, where the rites of Demeter, Persephone Kore and Necate were enacted, and as important as the oracular earth shrine of Gaia and Her Python priestesses at

Delphi. It must originally have been a women's sacred place where the rebirth of the ever-living Goddess from Herself was witnessed.

The promise of rebirth and immortality from the Universal Mother was symbolised by the rebirth of the corn each year. The Sumerian Inanna descends into the Underworld searching for Her child, Demeter mourns the disappearance of Her daughter into the Underworld and as a result all of Nature dies and becomes barren. Kore/Bride, who is Demeter/Cailleach's other and younger self, re-emerges at Imbolc and all of creation rejoices. What patriarchy has forgotten is that when the daughters are separated from each other and from the Mother/s all of Nature mourns and nothing will bear fruit. The Goddess was originally Herself the ruler of the Underworld, but in later times it was thought that Persephone was abducted, raped and forcibly made the wife of the king of Hades. Even then he had to allow Persephone/Kore to return to the Mother for six months of the year. At a later stage of patriarchy even this was no longer conceded. With the coming of bronze and the first Metal Age there emerged the belief in the sun as a male being, but at this early stage he was still thought to be born of the Mother within the temple/womb/tomb at sacred places like New Grange.

The Greek Festival of the Wild Women was held at the winter Solstice at Athens during which the death and rebirth of the harvest child Dionysus was enacted. Dionysus was torn apart and cannibalistically eaten by the nine women who represented the triads of the New, Full and Dark Moons. This appears to be a ritual going back as far as the Old Stone Age judging from an Aurignacian cave painting at Cogul[9]. The sun gods Dionysus, Apollo, Mithra and Christ were all reputedly born on the Winter Solstice. In ancient Syria and Egypt celebrants would retire into the inner shrines, from which they issued at midnight with a loud cry: "The Virgin (Inanna) has brought forth! The light is waxing!"[10]

In the south of Eire (Ireland is named after the Goddess Eire) there are the sacred mountains called the 'Paps of Anu' (Da Chích Anann). They are perfectly breast-shaped twin peaks on whose summits the ancients had built stone cairns to resemble nipples. The Celts appeared as a distinct tribal people from the Rhineland in Germany in the first millennium b.c. The earliest remnants of Celtic culture in Central Europe date back to between 800-450 b.c. From there they migrated in successive waves through Gaul to Spain, Italy and Greece. The Galicians in Northern Spain are Celts and apparently still practise some matrilocal customs to this day. It is thought that in the 5th century b.c. Celtic people of the Hallstadt Iron Age culture calling themselves the 'Sons of Mil' invaded Britain and occupied its south-eastern part. But some archaeologists believe that the first Celts already reached Ireland in the Bronze Age. They were an Indo-European warrior people thought to have brought their own male priesthood, the Druids, with them. Tall, blonde and well built, in contrast to the small dark Iberian peoples they invaded, they had already developed iron technology and cattle herding. They wielded large hacking swords and spears, drove fast two-horse chariots, built hill-forts and held control of trade routes between the Mediterranean, the West and the Middle East for almost a millennium. They were still, though, a tribal people holding land in common and regarding themselves as guardians of the Earth, the land belonging to the whole tribe by proxy of the Goddess. They practised matrilineal descent and took the name of the clan-Mother. The Celtic women were sexually and economically independent, owning property in their own right, often being heads of families and warriors renowned for their courage and skills in battle.

Their male gods were of recent origin, but their Goddesses were pre-Celtic and very ancient. Their war-Goddess Badh had triple aspects (Neman, Macha and Morrigu) and it was she who helped Queen Boadicea to victory against the Romans in a.d. 60 before her final defeat and suicide. The legendary warrior-queen, Maeve/Medb of Connacht, famous for her war chariots and courage in battle, might in fact have been a Goddess - of pride and sexual desire as well as of war. She is also called Mab, Queen of the Fairies, and her name means 'she who intoxicates'. The queens of Connacht might have personified her and assumed her name over the generations, since Connacht remained for long a stronghold of the matriarchal Iberian peoples.

The Celts seem to have embodied a strange mixture of Lunar insight and solar aggression. They combined ancient matriarchal beliefs in the Lunar/ Great Waters Goddess (Danu/Anu/Aine/ Cailleach/Brigid) with an emerging belief in an all-powerful Sun-god, Lugh, a kind of Celtic Apollo. The Sun was seen as the greatest warrior of all, the victor in the eternally renewed battle with the 'Serpent of Darkness'. The Indo-European idea of the Sun was of a celestial warrior-king drawn through the sky in a war chariot.

The introduction of the male-centred solar religion and calendar everywhere only reflected the interests of an emerging property-holding male ruling elite and was universally - in Egypt, Sumeria, India, and in pre-Columbian America - introduced by military force and priestly rule. The solar cult was invariably imposed from above and never arose spontaneously from the people, who everywhere persisted in their love of the Great Mother. The ancient priestesshoods of the Goddess, in Her many aspects, had to be rendered powerless and co-opted because they stood in the way of patriarchal economic interests and 'progress' towards increasing exploitation of the Earth's resources.

The Celts still had a Lunar time reckoning and realised that Light can only be born out of Darkness. The Irish ritual calendar began with Samhain, which was their New Year, at the end of October. In their conception of things Day was preceded by Night and the Goddess encompassed both the night- and the day-sky. All of Creation was born from the Dark Waters of 'Chaos'. The Celts never attempted to develop centralised city-states with all-powerful solar kings - and this is their saving grace.

With the new patriarchal belief in the Sun god as a sky-father and husband of a passive Earth Mother, it was no longer possible to conceive of him as a child born of the womb of the Mother at New Grange. This god was never born of a woman and like the Sun he never died. He was all-powerful and a law unto himself. The male priesthood now preached the anti-natural lie that the male Sun fertilized and brought into activity his own Mother the Earth and Her Underground Waters by means of his solar phallic beam. The son now begot his mother. What the Mother in the past had freely given out of Her own volition and love the son now tries to wrench from Her by force.

As we saw the Sun God is the warrior who battles eternally with the 'Serpent of Darkness' and overcomes Her with his phallic metal sword. The male 'hero' murders the Dragon/Serpent who is the Mother Goddess Tiamat of Babylon, Tehom of Israel or Delphyne of Greece. He also steals Her treasures and wealth in the caves and underground caverns. Remember the sagas of the Dragon who guards the treasure in the cave and who is slaughtered and robbed. The Dragon is the Earth Spirit and Her treasures are the minerals, ores and magnetic and healing Underground Waters. The myths of the hero who slays the Dragon/ Serpent/Monster are not just stories told symbolically about the destruction of the Goddess temples and the capture and rape of Her priestesses by patriarchal men: they are also accounts of the actual rape of the Earth. The ancient women Shamans had been the custodians of the healing waters, springs and wells of the Earth, and had believed that minerals correspond intimately with the planets that surround us. The Dragon/Serpent was as grey as the mud; She is Prima materia (materia/Mater/mother), golden as the Sun and multicoloured like the rainbow. She produces fire from Her breath, causes storms, winds and rain; She is the Milky Way and below Her chin She carries the Lunar pearl. She gives magic powers to those who are in tune with Her nature, and those who have accidentally tasted of Her blood can understand the language of birds and animals; she is the living waters within our own bodies and as Kundalini She slumbers at the base of our spines. When called upon, She travels through the centres of our bodies and gives illumination, magic powers and enlightenment; She is at one with our menstrual nature. *Charge of the Star Goddess*

In alchemy the Dragon represents the 'Place of Spirit', and the Dragon's 'fiery breath' signifies transmutation of matter through intense heat. John Michell writes of this: "The oldest branch of alchemy was concerned with bringing about the earthly paradise through the fruitful union of cosmic and terrestrial forces. Alchemy, astrology and geomancy originally united in a system that recognized correspondences between planetary influences and the Spirits of the Earth's salts."[12] Women had been the custodians of this ancient science and occult knowledge of sagic transformations, both in Nature and in our psyches. The new patriarchal solar myth, however, supplied the dominant males with the ideological justification for the pillaging and rape of the Earth in search of raw materials for the growing war and metal technologies.

It is significant I think that the modern symbol for 'male' is also the sign for the metal iron and for the war-god Mars. What is implied here is that only with warfare and metal technology did men become 'real men' – anti-Mother, sexually and economically dominant, and set on the conquest and destruction of Nature/Her. Without the incessant mining and smelting, especially of iron, men would not have been able to create imperialistic, centralised and warlike city-states. With iron weapons, and iron tools such as ploughs to rip the Earth open for agriculture on a large scale and axes for cutting down the vast forests, men could finally take over and impose their own anti-life values based on left-brain linear thinking. And furthermore, the belief that the Sky/Sun-father was the real creator of life and the passive Earth Mother (now devoid of her own regenerative, creative and magic powers) reduced to being simply his vessel to act upon, gave men, who had now broken out of tribal communistic shared living, the political and ideological justification for their acts. I believe that from the very beginnings of patriarchy (rule by the fathers) the disaster course was set towards our present industrial and capitalist society, a mechanical and soulless desacralized cosmos, a plundered and poisoned Earth. Without the minerals, without the exhaustive mining of coal and metals from within the belly of the Earth, we might not now be living on the brink of total destruction. The treasures of the Earth were tainted with the blood of the Dragon and what is taken from Her by force backfires on the violator and leads only to ruin. Even patriarchal men cannot actually live without their Mother, the Earth - and there is NO heavenly father to escape to.

The Celts, as we saw, were still a tribal people and originally their clan-Mother was the White Goddess, giver of rebirth, of poetic and magic powers[13]. She was embodied by the Queen of Elphame - the Fairy Queen of the ancient people - and the sacred king as Her consort and son who took the part of the dying year-god of vegetation. Near the Boyne Valley temples is Tara Hill, ancient sacred centre of the four provinces of Ireland. Here the Celtic chieftains were crowned and sacrifices made at Samhain/Halloween to the spirits of those who had died during the previous year. Bridget Morgan says of this: "The Indo-European theme of the divine king mated to the Earth Goddess who represented the sovereignty of the kingdom was re-enacted at Tara, where the high king's coronation ritual was called his 'wedding feast'. The Goddess was present in the form of the hill of Tara, as a mare or fawn, as a young girl on a throne, or an old woman who turns into a young maiden after being united with the king, just as the new king was believed to restore youth and vigour to the land."[14]

Tara is also a pre-Celtic hill/mound and is cut through underground with tunnels, chambers and burrows. It is believed that the Fairies - 'the little people' - live here inside the hill. No local person will go near here at night. Tara is a famous tourist place, but interestingly enough we found that on the four ancient Quarter Days of the year (Imbolc, Beltane, Lammas and Samhain) it was shut off to the public. It is believed that on those sacred days of high energies the Fairies are celebrating at Tara. Or is it that we are being prevented from celebrating the ancient festivals at this particularly sacred site?

It is very likely that the 'Fairy folk' were the people of the heath, the small, dark aboriginal people who were displaced by the Celts. They were believed to live in the mounds and barrows belonging to an earlier culture. Their queen was the White Goddess, giver of immortality and transmutation. They were thought to raise power through circular dancing at night-time amongst the sacred stones and barrows and to possess great magic skills. At those times auras of light were seen and haunting music heard.

The 'Fairies' bred cattle in the hills, lived in turf-covered huts and preserved the old Religion of the Stones, Moon and Waters. They celebrated the eight Feasts of the Wheel with wild dances, processions and ritual fires. There was a lot of intermingling and intermarriage between the Celts and the Fairy folk and many 'traditional Witches' in Ireland believed themselves to have been taught by the 'Fairies' and to have had 'Fairy blood' in the family. 'Fairy' later became another word for 'Witch'. In Scotland during the 'Burning Times' any communication with Fairies was taken as an admission of dealings with Witches.

Theories have been put forward that the 'Sidh' - the tall 'Shining Ones' - were another kind of spirit-being of the Otherworld and were also thought to live in the earthworks and mounds, in places like New Grange; that they are immortal and exist in a halfway state between this world and the next. It is possible that they were originally a Neolithic people highly skilled in magic and psychic powers, that perhaps they were the creators of the Boyne Valley culture and were later deified by other Neolithic peoples. The 'Sidh' in their turn seem to have defeated peoples called the Fir-Bolgs and Fomors. The People of the Sidh (Fairy folk) had called themselves Tuatha dé Danann, which means the 'Children of the Goddess Danu'. Danu/Anu/Bride/ Cailleach was also seen as the ancestral Mother of the Celts who believed themselves to be reincarnations of the People of the Sidh. The 'Shining Ones' became confused in more recent times with the small, dark people - the 'Fairy people' of the heaths.[15]

On the summit of Tara Hill stands a sculpture of St. Patrick. It is said that it was here that he drove the 'Serpents' from Ireland, meaning that he defeated the Druids' magic with his own brand of christian magic, called 'miracles'. I left a blooded sanitary towel at his feet just to let him know exactly what I think of his presence here on Her ancient and sacred mound.

On the edges of Tara there is a christian church. Here, as on many other of Her sacred places and mounds the christians have tried to nullify or to co-opt Her powers to their own advantage. But in the graveyard surrounding the church we discovered a standing stone with a very faded 'Sheela-na-gig' image carved on it. These strange and powerful images of the Goddess reduced to Her most naked abstraction as a grinning skull and holding Her cunt wide open with both hands are found widely all over the Celtic world even on and in medieval churches and castles. She was the Mother of All and the Guardian of the Otherworld and must originally have been placed above the door or gateways early Celtic Culdee church. These churches were an attempt at combining the beliefs of the old Religion with christianity.[16] Prophesy, divination and magic of all kinds were common in Ireland and some of the Culdee priesthood were still practising Druids. St. Patrick, who had arrived on his mission to Ireland in a.d. 432, and other early christians, had Christ wedded to the Goddesses of Ireland and saw him as the newest heroic embodiment of the warrior god.

These male priests were not celibate, and priestesses - the Conhospitae - assisted in the mass and administered the wine while the male priests distributed the wafers. Under Celtic law women had far greater rights than present-day British or Irish women. Ireland was never conquered either by the Romans or the Saxons and Druidism thrived there much longer than in Britain. Because the Culdee church included much druidic teaching it was therefore a threat to the patriarchal and authoritarian catholic church which was set on its drive for imperialistic spiritual and economic control over the peoples of Europe.

At the Synod of Drunceat held in 574 a.d. the Druids were finally stripped of their special privileges as administrators of the people and as priests of the old Religion in Ireland. In 597 St. Augustine brought papal christianity to Britain, which was by then extensively settled by Angles, Saxons and Jutes, although Sussex resisted the cross until a.d. 681, in 553 the Council of Constantinople had declared the Doctrine of Reincarnation to be heresy. By this they wanted to - in a single stroke - defeat the Gnostic sects as well as the followers of the religion of the Goddess of Rebirth and Life after Death. The catholic priests were, during this time, also seriously discussing whether women could be said to possess an immortal soul! According to them we are at a lower stage of development and of animal nature... The catholic hierarchy preaches that animals are not ensouled. It seems that at a European synod where this matter was to be settled it was only thanks to a few Celtic bishops who decided in favour of women that there was a one vote majority for our souls! In the Ancient Religion all of the Earth, with its animal and plant life, its stones and waters, was experienced as sacred and of the essence of the living breathing being of the Mother. Not so with patriarchal religions like Christianity which see their godhead as a disembodied abstract spirit-being on high.

As late as 607 a.d. the Celtic church refused to acknowledge the supremacy of Rome. They were, however, forced into submission at the hands of the combined forces of the catholic priesthood and the military might of the Saxons and Angles who hated the Celts and wanted to see their downfall. It seems that Welsh Culdee bishops and priests were lured treacherously to their deaths and that the ancient library at Bangor in North Wales, with its invaluable Celtic manuscripts, was burnt to the ground. This was so according to Gerald Gardner in his book 'The Meaning of Witchcraft', written in the 1950s.[17]

In the 7th century Theodore forbad the practice in the christian world of dancing in animal masks, especially those of horned beasts. And so it went on, with the church becoming increasingly oppressive the more it consolidated its power until in the 15th century it felt itself strong enough to begin large scale persecution and mass genocide of those still practising the old Religion.

The masked dances imitating horned beasts had been partaken of by women and men Shamans since times immemorial. They had still been practised in trance-states during which the participants became as one with the Horned Goddess and Her son/lover Cernunnos, the horned stag god of the hunt, amongst the Celts.

With papal supremacy in the Celtic world - especially in Ireland - came the downfall of the free and independent Celtic women. Even today Irish women are under the stranglehold of the roman catholic church and under the thumb of its celibate male priesthood. This is ironic considering women's powerful position in Ireland in past ages. Of course English Imperialism, poverty, economic exploitation and hardship have much to answer for too.

This summer - in July 1982 - I revisited southern Ireland and returned once more to New Grange, Knowth and Dowth, and to Tara Hill. Maggie Lannin, my feminist artist friend in Dublin, had already in 1978 given me a book about the Sheela-na-gig images.[18] Now I found that Maggie was working in the National Museum in Dublin, in the basement of which there are about ten stone carvings of the Sheela that are only gathering the dust. They are not on public display because they are thought of as being offensive and obscene! Maggie was able to take me down into the basement to see the images...and powerful and moving they are too. They are an important part of our women's heritage and should be displayed in a Museum of Women's Culture, Herstory and Art.

It was our journey to Ireland in 1978 and our discovery of the Sheela-na-gig carvings and our powerful experience of New Grange that had inspired Marika and I to put our exhibition 'Woman-Magic, Celebrating the Goddess Within Us' on the road in December of that year. The image of the Sheela became the symbol for the exhibition and it has appeared on all our posters and catalogues and inspired some of our own work. It is interesting that my painting 'God Giving Birth' (1968) is, like the Sheela-na-gig, considered by some people to be 'offensive' and 'obscene' (and also 'blasphemous'), and has nearly landed me in court many times. When I did this painting I was completely unaware of the Sheela-na-gig images. Our exhibition has travelled since the Winter of 1978 to nine different cities in England, has recently been shown in Germany, and is, at the time of writing, in Scandinavia where it is being described as an exhibition of 'Images from Ancient Celtic Womencultures'[19]. Although I am originally Swedish, I realise when returning to Germanic countries just how profoundly I have been changed and transformed by living in these Isles - with their still living remnants of Neolithic and Celtic culture - for half a lifetime. Being in Wales for nearly four years has also deeply influenced me. And by the way, the Welsh national emblem/flag is a red Dragon on a green background - which could well be a living reminder of the matriarchal past.

THE FAIRY TRADITION AND THE CRAFT

Wales was renowned for its 'witchcraft' and its poetry, the traditional folk dress of Welsh women being, according to popular imagination, the classic witch's outfit complete with black top hat, while the bards were devotees of their Muse - the White Goddess. Among the Welsh there are still many great poets and singers.

As we have discussed, the Celts were a warlike Indo-European Iron Age people who didn't arrive from central Europe until ca. 500 b.c. Through intermarriage with the ancient people (the Fairy folk) and through the powerful and magic influence exerted by the sacred stones, wells, mounds and temples of the Neolithic Goddess, the Celts were, I believe, like myself profoundly changed and transformed.

Shamanistic priestesshoods of the aboriginal and ancient peoples were the custodians of the magic sacred tradition, knowledge and learning. Gerald Gardner, who was an anthropologist and an initiated witch, founded many covens in Britain in the 1950s when the remaining laws against the Craft and Spiritualism had been finally removed from the statute book. He says that the Druids were initiated and taught some of the knowledge and science of astrology and of the Megalithic stones by these extremely mysterious women. Coming from the 'Fairy race' they were the guardians of the Mysteries and intermediaries with the Otherworld, the Spiritworld of the Goddess, the Nether World that can still be experienced within the chambers of New Grange.

Jean Markale[20], who wrote 'Women of the Celts', speaks of mysterious Pictish Amazon/lesbian priestesshoods living in the Scottish Highlands who practised ritual sexual magic and who even initiated famous and legendary Celtic warrior-heroes. Perhaps these women were the priestesses of the triple war-Goddess Badh, or of the Morrigan, which means 'Great Queen'. She might have originally been the Dark Mother of the Tombs, perhaps being transformed into the warrior-Goddesses flying over the battlefields in the form of a Black Raven when Her people, the Iberians, desperately tried to defend their land and culture from the invading Celts and the Sons of Mil. Like the Hindi Goddess Kali She brings destruction and terror. She lives on in the popular imagination and is still to this day dreaded as the Banshee (Bean-Sidhe), the Fairy tomb-woman who warns members of old Irish families of impending death.

The Otherworld was called 'the land of everliving women' and most of the Fairies were in fact women. In Wales their queen was called Gwenhidw, which means White Lady. In the Celtic legends, though, the Goddesses became guardians and Fairy-lovers of the male heroes, and that appears to be their main function. King Arthur's queen was called Gwenhyvar, which means 'White Apparition'. It is quite likely that she was still the White Goddess and Arthur Her sacred king. There are many myths of priestesshoods living, without men, on sacred and remote islands where they practise healing, divination, prophesy and magic.

The People of the Sidhe - the Tuatha dé Danann or 'Fairy Women' - were thought to direct the magnetic currents of the Earth. They are said to live on islands far out at sea and in Fairy mounds, caves and caverns; they rule the Feast of the Dead - Samhain - and are in control of all the spirits of the Dead who are then at large. They control the ripening of the crops and the milkgiving of the cows; they are also Goddesses of the Harvest and are seen chiefly at night frequenting forests and fountains. The Fairy Queen who watches over cows is called Gruagach and in the Scottish Highlands women pour libations of milk to Her on sacred stones that are called Leac na Cruagaich (Flagstones of the Gruahach). They were believed to be the indwelling spirits of the sacred stones and were thought to be a sort of magnetic fluid or aura. Healing powers were attributed to them and it was believed that the magic fluid or aura could be transmitted by the laying on of hands and by magic passes on the nape of the neck or along the dorsal spine of the patient.

It was believed that rocks set in motion by the spirits animating them sometimes went to the rivers to drink. Thirty 'rocking stones' have been found in Britain. It is popularly thought that sacred stones cannot be counted: they never add up. In the romances many of the Welsh and Irish heroes fall in love with Fairy women and follow them to Avalon, the Otherworld of sacred apple groves. The magic wand and the silver branch with three golden apples belong to the Fairy Queen/Goddess, as does the Cauldron of Regeneration and Rebirth and the food-giving Fountain of Annwn (Under-Well-Land). 'To die' simply meant to go on the journey to the 'Land of the Living', also called the 'Happy Plain' and the 'Land of Promise'. In Wales it was called 'Tir-na-gog', the 'Land of

Youth', and was thought to lie beyond the ocean in the 'Isles of the Blessed' which have been lost to us.

The Bean-Sidhe/Banshee/Wailing Woman is in places identified with Aine/Anu. I picked up this account about Her in W. Y. Evans Wentz's book 'The Fairy Faith in Celtic Countries' (1911): There is an ancient place of initiation, an Otherworld preserve with Fairy-Goddesses who dwell both in the lake and on the hills surrounding it at Lough (Lake) Gur in County Limerick. Beneath the waters of the lake is believed to be one of the chief entrances to the Fairy realm. Every seven years the lake dries up and a tree is seen growing from its bed. The tree is covered with a green cloth and under it sits the lake's guardian, a woman knitting. In the myth it is said that the lake was originally a well but because of the guardian woman's carelessness it overflowed. There are two hills by Lough Gur upon whose summits sacrifices and sacred sites used to be celebrated according to living tradition. They are called 'Knock Aine' or 'Ane' (as we saw AN means heavenly and bright) and 'Knock Fennel', Hill of the Goddess Fennel. 'Fennel' comes from 'finnen' which means 'white'. According to legend Aine, like the Breton Morgan, may sometimes be seen combing Her hair with a golden comb, one half of Her body above the lake. When the water is clear one may see beneath Aine's lake the enchanted castle of Her son Geriod who lives there. Once every seven years on clear moonlit nights he emerges temporarily on a phantom white horse leading Fairies across the land.

It was also commonly believed that a man is drowned in the lake every seven years and that it is the Beann Fhionn or White Lady who takes him. Aine's true dwelling place is in Her hill upon which on every Summer Solstice night the peasantry used to gather to view the Moon, then with torches made of bunches of straw and hay tied on poles they marched in procession from the hill and ran through the cultivated fields and among the cattle so as to increase the fertility in Nature. The Goddess Herself was seen to be leading the procession. The peasants said that Aine "is the best-hearted woman that ever lived". With the slow takeover by patriarchal male gods Aine became identified with the Wailing Woman/Bainshee.

> Aine from Her closely hid nest did awake,
> the woman of wailing/keening from Gur's voicy lake.

She is supposed to appear sitting on an ancient earthen monument shaped like a great chair on 'Knock Adoon' (Hill of the Fort) which juts into the lake. Aine is also a Fairy Queen.

I find this account extremely interesting. It seems to me that here are all the elements of the Mysteries of the Goddess. Here are Her Sacred Waters, Well and Lake, and the Hill/Mound where she dwells. She is also the Goddess as the Tree of Life and the Entrance to the Otherworld, as well as the Dark Mother/old Hag who is guardian of both. Before there were the Neolithic stone circles there were always trees and mountains. Sacred trees and mountains were seen as the Navel of the Earth from where all creation originates and where all the realities where seen to merge. The Goddess was the Tree of Life. The Tree grows every seven years, upon which the phantom white horse and rider appear and a man is drowned in the lake, taken by the 'White Lady'. The number seven is a sacred Lunar number and the number of the coils of the underwater geodetic Spirals. One of the forms of the Goddess is as a White Mare and in this aspect She is called Epona or Rhiannon. She is as white as the moonlight, the sea-foam and the chalklands of the south of England, where Her form can be found cut in the turf of various hillsides.

Here is the triple Goddess - Aine, Fennel and the old woman Guardian of the Lake, and here also is an account of a celebration and ritual on the night of the Summer Solstice. The ritual is clearly Lunar in nature and is thought to increase fertility in plants and cattle. I'm sure that very similar celebrations were performed at Silbury Mound, Glastonbury Tor, and at many other of Her sacred places in the Neolithic world. The male Greek god Dionysus, who took over many of the rites of the Cretan Mother and Her ecstatic women-followers, was still thought to lead the sacred torch-light processions in the night. And of course in patriarchal times the Goddess becomes the 'Wailing Woman', lamenting the destruction of the Earth, the pollution of Her Waters, the rape of Her Body, Her lost Daughters. All she is left with is sorrow and the power to predict death. This overwhelming grief is what I myself so strongly experienced on Silbury, which is Her pregnant Belly. Tears are what women inherit in father-ruled societies, and this will continue to be so until the Daughters rise again, together and in love for our Mother.

Spirit of the Stones (1980). (Probably inspired by the sarsens at Avebury)

The womenshamans were village priestesses and healers of the common people, as were the later Witches who inherited their tradition and knowledge and worshipped the Moon at night within the stone circles. The Craft/old Religion was the religion of the soil, while Druidism was that of the aristocracy and the rulers. Gerald Gardner says that the Druids were the priesthood of the Sun, that they were civil servants, educators, politicians, and the hidden hand that ruled the king or chieftain. They were attempting to usurp Matriarchy and to take over the exercise of power from women. In time they became the custodians of vision, prophesy, sacrifice, lore, the ritual calendar and the law. Every Druid was also a bard and had to train for many years to memorise the oral traditions and laws that were handed down, and continuously added to, in complicated verse. The oral traditions lived on longest in Ireland and only in the 9th century a.d. did Irish monks begin to transcribe the oral tales. The Druids knew, from the women Shamans, how to enter the

Otherworld in trance states and how to shape-shift. They were physicians with a great knowledge of herbs, which had always been since times immemorial a women's sphere. The priestesses of the Goddess had always also been midwives and healers; the first temples had been the precincts within which the women gave birth. The Druids also made incantations and practised divination and charms[21]. They worshipped in oak groves ('Dru' means oak, and Druid means 'oak-knower'), on hilltops and by lakesides, using a secret Ogham alphabet based on the lore and magic of trees.

The Celts were a strange people who understood collective dream states where past and present, psychic and physical realities merge, who excelled in in-between states and twilight zones. They were anti-dualistic and still worshipped Nature and were at one with Her animals and plants, believing in reincarnation - the spiralling journey into the Still Centre of the Goddess and back out again - and thought of death as but the centre of a long life. But they were at times also head hunters said to practise mass sacrifices and the men believed it to be the greatest honour to die in battle. This is also what the Vikings thought and practised. The Celts believed in an ever-changing world in which nothing is as it first appears: they loved ambiguity.

The Druids, however, incited the British to resistance against the Roman invaders and for this they were punished. A great number of Druids were trapped by the Romans in their centre of Mona in Anglesey at the northern tip of Wales in 60 a.d., there to be slaughtered. This finally broke their power. The unofficial priestesshoods of the ancient peoples had gone largely unnoticed by the Romans according to Gerald Gardner, and he says that they survived underground to later re-emerge as the latterday Wicce or Witches. So it comes to be that some present-day covens claim an unbroken tradition handed down through many generations of mothers and daughters all the way back to the Neolithic Faery folk. This may or may not be so... I feel though that surely much of what is thought of as 'Craft tradition' is more Celtic than Neolithic. The use of iron tools and utensils - knife, sword and cauldron - by many covens is surely of Iron Age origin. Iron was detested by the Fairies and according to some dowsers[22] it interrupts the flow of the Earth Spirit and disturbs the subtle magnetic currents that are ruled by the Lunar Mother.

On the sacred island of Malta no tools or weapons made of metal have been found at all. It is also a mystery how the people there built the many and gigantic oracular Goddess temples and the enormous underground catacombs, the Cities of the Dead watched over by the owl-faced Tomb Mother. Of course the local myth tells of how they were built in one night by a giant woman with a baby at Her breast. Did the ancient women Shamans know of some form of psychic technology by which they could lift gigantic stones and literally 'move mountains'...? Could they, for example, tap into some pitch of sound by which they could affect the very nature and structure of matter? Remember the young singing women and the stone circles in Cornwall. Anyway, on Malta any form of metal appears to have been strictly taboo, although in later times there were Bronze Age cultures in the Mediterranean contemporary with the Maltese sacred and timeless Neolithic temples.[23]

The priestesses on Malta were the oracles and healers to the surrounding peoples and were finely tuned to 'the voices of the Underworld', gaining their prophetic and healing knowledge in dream/trance states within the underground womb chambers of the Goddess. They were in tune with the magnetic Earth-current and their knowledge and magic was based on its undisturbed flow.

The great emphasis, within the Craft tradition, on the male horned god Cernunnos, stag god of the hunt, is also part of the Celtic tradition from what I understand, and does not belong with the Neolithic peoples.[24]

Though the ancient magic beliefs and practices persisted for a long time among the common people, and women in Saxon times had a high standing in society, the up-and-coming Saxon and later Viking rulers gradually introduced worship of patriarchal warrior-gods like Odin and Thor, who had by now lost any trace of their shamanistic nature and become thoroughly respectable. In Norse religion the ancient Mother and Daughter Goddess Nerthus/Freya taught Odin and the later male gods and their priesthood shamanism. The priestesses of Freya practised 'Sejd' which was the shamanistic art of entering into ecstatic trance states and communing with the Spirits and the Dead. This inspired state was seen to be "dangerous and chaotic and uncontrollable" by later male priesthoods set on introducing 'law and order' and organising the beginnings of patriarchal states and hierarchic class structures. The new rulers of England hated the Celts and feared their magic. They began making laws against the aboriginal magic, against those skilled in casting spells, against worshippers of the Dead and those who communicated with trees and stones who could project their astral bodies. There were attempts to forbid divining by the Moon, worshipping rivers, wells, stones and trees. The Gaelic and Brythonic magicians, Witches and 'Fairy mediums' always claimed to derive their powers from their ability to communicate with Fairies, Spirits and the Dead. Through them they could reveal the past, foretell the future, cast spells, perform exorcisms and control the weather and other natural phenomena. The Druids were thought to interpret the secret will of the Fairies. Witches are embodied spirits who have the ability to act in conjunction with disembodied spirits through the employment of occult forces. Magic was simply the supreme science and knowledge of how to be in contact with the unseen animate and intelligent forces that guide our lives.

'Wicce Craft' was a name coined by the Saxons to refer apparently to 'bending and shaping'. The Germanic leaders of the Saxons detested the visionary, poetic and fantastic bent of the Celtic imagination. There is still today something of this difference and hostility between the 'practical and rational English' and the 'crazy and wayward Celts' and this was also the difference I sensed when returning with the 'Woman-Magic' exhibition to my Germanic homelands. Wherever there are still surviving magical and shamanistic 'natural peoples' - such as the Samis of the north of Scandinavia, the Eskimos/ Inuits of Greenland, the tribal peoples of Siberia, the native peoples of North and South America, the Ainus of Japan, the Dravids of India, the Bushpeople of southern Africa and the Aborigines of Australia - western imperialist countries, especially the USA, are busy destroying their cultures. As still living custodians of the Earth (the native Americans talk constantly of the Earth as 'our Mother' that we must not damage), they are trying to protect their ancient sacred ancestral burial grounds from rape and pillage by the mining companies and pose a threat to the anti-natural, perverse and death-worshipping cultures of the alienated fathers. This is not to say, however, that some of these 'natural peoples' have not themselves developed many patriarchal and anti-women practices over the millennia.

I recently heard Shorty O'Neil of the Aboriginal Commission to Europe speaking about present-day uranium mining and British nuclear bomb testing in the 1950s in Australia. He also spoke of American testing of atomic bombs on islands in the Pacific and their deliberate disregard for the lives of native peoples who are or have been used as radiation guinea pigs. The Aboriginal peoples are granted as few rights as are animals in these societies. O'Neil said that the underground waterways of the Earth are the blood vessels of Her Body and that if the waters are interfered with in one place a whole forest fed by the waters might die many miles away, that radiation discharged into the waters from the uranium mines poisons all the streams, and is carried very far underground and finally out into the oceans which are dying as a result.

He also said that the Aboriginal peoples consider themselves the guardians of the Earth where they were born and where they also want to die, that we are here to cherish the sacred land and take care of Her, that if we die far away from our own ancestral burial grounds we will become lost spirits and will not be received back into her. The Aborigines believe in reincarnation and want to see a land to be reborn back into. The nuclear scientists and the US government are gambling not only with out present lives and with the coming generations, but also with our souls and our bodies of rebirth through our Mother the Earth for all eternity. How dare they...

All the Celtic countries - Wales, Ireland, the Isle of Man, the West of Scotland, Cornwall and Britanny - were all joined culturally and spiritually at one time, just as they were connected ethnically and linguistically. On the Isle of Man the mysteries of the sea-god Manannan were practised. This male god's name sounds suspiciously like the ancient name of the Goddesses Anu, Danu and Anna. In fact Aine was supposed to have been his 'wife'! The sea was always the original Mother.

JOURNEY TO BRITANNY

In the summer of 1979 we travelled to Brittany (Bretagne), which was
anciently called Armorica or 'Land of the Sea'; another centre of the
Megalithic culture of the Celtic world. We headed for Carnac, down
south in the Bay of Morbihan. Carnac means 'Place of Cairns or Tumuli'
and is the sacred centre of Brittany, just as Tara is the sacred centre of
Ireland. Unusual happenings or strange accidents and deaths are often
attributed in Ireland to Fairy interference, whilst in Brittany they are said
to be due to the influence of the Dead. The Breton world of the Dead,
like the Land of the Fairie or Otherworld, may be underground, in the
air, inside a hill or mountain or on an island out at sea. The Breton
people of the past made no distinction between the Living and the Dead,
believing that the Dead can make themselves visible to us and possess a
kind of body; that they, like the Fairies, can strike down the Living.

According to Breton belief the soul is supposed to depart from the body
during dreams, trances and times of ecstasy, see spirits of all kinds in
another world and be under their influence. Ankou was their king of the
Dead and his subjects had their own particular paths and roads - 'Fairy
paths' of the underground serpentine water currents - on which they
travelled in great sacred processions like the Greek Goddess Hecate and
Her companies of the dead spirits. Both the Fairies and the Dead had
their festivities at Samhain during which the Living prepared a feast for
them and mortal musicians played for the invisible crowds. Libations of
milk were poured onto the ancestral tombs in the same way as milk was
poured to the Fairy women and the Goddess on the standing stones and
capstones of the cromlechs of Ireland and Wales. The Fairy folk of
Brittany were the Corrigans, who could be either tiny and transparent
women or a race of dwarfs, the ancient people of the caves. They were
also thought of as souls-in-pain, condemned to wander at night in
wasteland and marsh. The Fairy women dwelt in fountains and wells, in
caves and dolmens, in grottoes in the sea-cliffs. They guarded hidden
treasure and danced the Breton 'ronde', a circular dance of initiation, at
Full Moon by menhirs and dolmens, at tumuli and at crossroads. Where
they dance their ring-dances mushrooms are said to grow. This summer I
found one such small perfect circle of mushrooms by a very ancient
forest in Sweden where they are called 'Witches circles'.

54

The Fairy women are also called Fées or 'Bonnes Dames' and they also appear as little old women known as 'Grac'hed Coz'. Associated with them is a legend of the dreaded 'Phantom Washerwomen of the Night', women condemned for ever to wash their own shrouds. In Ireland and Scotland the 'Banshee' (the Goddess) wails before a death; in Wales the 'Death Candle' (a disembodied ball of light seen floating in the air) is seen; in Britanny Ankou sounds a doleful cry before the door of the one he calls. There was also another kind of Fairy women - the Morgans - who lived in the waters and were thought to lure men to their death. They were manifestations of the ancient Sea Goddess whose embrace means death to patriarchal men and who often take the form of a swan. The Breton women's traditional headdress is very tall, white-laced and conical. Is it, like the Welsh women's black top hat a matriarchal remain?

The Celts believed that Carnac was the place from where the heroes set out on their journey to the Isles of the Blest. At Carnac there is row upon row of stones that march shoulder to shoulder across the landscape for miles on end. North-east of this little sea town there are three areas including nearly three thousand stones and a number of tombs extending for some five miles. There are three alignments called Menec, Kermario and Kerlescan, running roughly north-east to south-west. Each alignment is a vast processional avenue of at first small stones, then rising to greater and greater heights, culminating in semi-circles of huge slabs, sacred areas within which mysterious rites must once have taken place. Mont St. Michael nearby is one of the largest burial mounds in Europe. Note that the christians built a church dedicated to St. Michael, the arch-Dragonslayer, on its top. Churches dedicated to this 'saint' and 'archangel' were everywhere built on Her sacred Dragon Mounds in Britain, especially in Cornwall. Every day for four days we walked along the alignments, experiencing their mystery and power. The Stones are thought to be the abode of the Corrigans and are regarded as endowed with and enveloped by mysterious life. The ghosts of the Dead are said to haunt the avenues after nightfall. There is a Morbihan legend that they are Pagan Roman soldiers who were turned into stone by St. Cornely in retribution for having persecuted him. He is the patron saint of Brittany who presides over the alignments and the domestic horned animals. It would seem as if St. Corneley is a christianised version of the Celtic god Cernunnos - the horned god.

The Horned Goddess (Cow Goddess) and Her son the bullcalf were perhaps thought to be the indwelling deities of the Stones. A small statue of a bronze cow was found near Carnac. The great Goddess Brigid/Bride, also christianised as St. Brigid, presided over the crops, the animal herds and the world of Nature. On the eve of Imbolc/Bride's Day (February lst) She 'does her rounds' with Her white milk-cow, who is the Lunar side of Her nature[25], and offerings of grain are placed outside the houses for Her. In the Morbihan on the night of the Summer Solstice a great fire was lit in the middle of the main road and covered with green branches to produce plenty of smoke. The animals were driven through the smoke and fire to protect them from illness and evil spirits and to ensure a good milk supply. At Carnac on the 13th of September an annual fête was held in honour of St. Cornely. All the animals were blessed or exorcised with holy water at the church door. In St. Cornely's fountain is a Pagan holy well. Here seems to have been the remains of a cult of the cattle. Originally the Goddess was the herd, the enclosure for the herds and its sacred gateway.[26]

The largest stone pillar still standing in Brittany is the 36 foot high menhir of Kerloas, near Plouharzel in Finistère. Other pillars between 21 and 30 feet in height are not unusual and many of them are aligned with standing stones in Cornwall. The 'Stone of the Fairies' (El Grah), which is now sadly broken, was originally 67 feet long and weighed over 340 tons. It was apparently used to predict Lunar eclipses, as well as the major and minor Lunar standstills and the amount of perturbation from monuments and coastal points up to ten miles away. In the passage graves one finds the grim face of the Tomb Mother, called 'La Grande Mere'.

Some of the menhirs are said to have fertility in their gift. Earlier this century women still went secretly to one or the other of the menhirs of St. Cado near Ploemel to rub themselves against certain parts of the stone, regarding this as a sure method of ensuring early pregnancy. A number of free standing Megalithic tombs, known as 'hot stones', were used in a similar way. At certain phases of the Moon girls who wanted husbands had to sit on or slide down these tombs naked. The tombs at Locmariaquer are reputed to have been especially effective and at the beginning of May they were adorned with coloured ribbons and kerchiefs. Up until the last century the church fought the 'obscene practices' associated with the ancient stones and monuments and until recently wives of seamen used to tap the 'cup marks' on the stone of a corbelled tomb near Carnac with a hammer. They did this to obtain good winds for their men's ships or a change of the weather, believing

56

that winds are spirits of the Dead who control the weather, cure and heal. In a French church near Bourg a large stone was preserved "into which the sick and impotent grind holes and then drink the pulverised matter". They believe it cures fevers and renews strength. Also water produced on holy stones - in its hollows - was seen as healing and possessing miraculous powers. "Cup marks' in other places are used by sick people to 'blow away' their illnesses. They literally blow into the marks on the stones.

The Goddess at Carnac 1980

The Corrigans, who were thought to inhabit or dwell in the stones at Carnac, were said to be very small, but having a tremendous strength they could lift huge boulders. They wore white linen and were great weavers as well as great sorceresses and can be seen at particular phases of the Moon when they dance around dolmens in certain fields. These places are indicated by dark patches were it is not a good idea to tread.

I know of two women who some years ago went on a Full Moon night to the Stones at Carnac, bringing with them a wooden mallet. One of the women hit one of the largest stones, situated at a ritual centre, with the mallet. Apparently the stone made a hollow sound like a bell and this carried on down the line of stones behind it. The women repeated the action to establish that they were not imagining things. When the same thing happened again they became suddenly fearful and felt themselves as if surrounded by thousands of silent (possibly threatening) beings in the moonlight. They left in a hurry with the feeling that they might have been tampering with energies they might not be able to handle. Are the stone alignments some kind of vast conductor of energies, a cosmic musical instrument, or what?

Francis Hitching in 'Earth Magic' [27] says that Carnac, together with Stonehenge, can be seen as a "vast experimental laboratory for testing and refining the procedures of Lunar observation". According to some dowsers there are powerful underground water energy-lines running beneath the stone alignments. It was thought that the Stones at Carnac went to the waters to drink on Yuletide Eve. Similar stories are told of other standing stones.

The difficulties involved in carrying out Lunar observations for the small communistic and matrilinear farming communities must have been enormous and the time-scale so vast that it can only have been done for overwhelming religious and practical reasons. Women were the ancient farmers and had brought about the Neolithic 'revolution' through their discovery that food producing plants can be grown and harvested regularly. It appears that the whole of Neolithic culture depended on these Lunar observations. According to Hitching it is infinitely more difficult to study the orbit of the Moon than that of the Earth around the Sun. Unlike the Sun, the Moon describes an arc round the Earth that is not the same from month to month: it is slightly tilted in such a way that over a period of 18.6 years, corresponding to the magic number 19 - every nineteen years the Lunar beam enters New Grange - then gradually moves its rising and setting points further inwards from these extreme points, and after 9.3 years (the magic number 9) begins to move back again. This must have been very difficult to study and work out since it would have been necessary to be able to study the Moon through more than one complete nineteen year cycle to be able to establish a repeating cycle.

A. Thom has found that at more than two dozen stone circle sites Neolithic peoples established to within a few degrees the eight declinations that mark the extreme points of the Moon's swing. The extreme positions they had discovered, when the Moon each 9.3 years begins to turn around and retrace its steps at Moonrise and Moonset, are known as the major and minor standstills. It is only for a few days on either side of these standstills that it is possible to make an observation of another peculiarity of the Moon's orbit - the tiny wobble, or perturbation, that runs on a cycle of 173.3 days. This movement is so slight, being less than one third of a degree in total, that until recently it was thought to have been undiscovered until the end of the 16th century. But it is crucial because it is only when perturbation is around its largest that eclipses can occur. Megalithic peoples could measure this wobble and this means that they were able to predict such eclipses. These Lunar observations were of great mystical and navigational importance. But I have nowhere as yet come across a good explanation of why Lunar eclipses in particular had such tremendous and magical significance to Neolithic peoples.

Gerald Hawkins suggested in 1963 that most of the twelve major astronomical alignments - four solar and eight Lunar - could be found in the geometry of Stonehenge. He also suggested that the fifty-six 'Aubrey holes' were almost exactly three times the 18.61 year cycle of the Moon and were used to predict Lunar eclipses; that Stonehenge is an excellent predictor of eclipses. Thom suggests that Stonehenge was so positioned that distant hills align astronomically with the great stone arches. Scientists are baffled at how the ancients were able to stake out the Lunar positions (using wooden posts and ropes). A Lunar standstill occurs only twice in eighteen years. Also we don't know how they passed on this information through the generations. Martin Brennan thinks, though, that within the stone carvings at New Grange and other sacred temples there is encoded mathematical and astronomical knowledge. I also think that the symbols used on the pots (and women were the ancient potters) was a sacred sign language through which much information could be communicated.

The Sun moves across to the right (if in the North) for half a year, until it reaches a point where it apparently sets in the same place for about a week (at the Summer Solstice); then it moves slowly leftwards until six months later it again appears to wait at its furthest point for a week (Midwinter Solstice) before turning back and retracing its steps to the right again. The Sun is predictable in a way which the Moon isn't. The equinoxes are the times when days and nights have the same number of hours. The ancients measured the risings and settings of Moon and Sun using mountain peaks as foresights, coordinated the agricultural and astronomical year and worked out four-weekly Lunar cycles. They studied the stars and knew that the forces of the Earth and the planets affect each other. They understood much better than we do today that all things are subject to minute and almost undetectable changes of influence and live within cycles and rhythms: they knew the inseparable unity of all things.

There are suggestions of electric currents near the Earth's core that might create Her magnetic field. Apparently there have been unexplained changes in the Earth's polarities - the direction of the Earth's magnetic field - in the past, which are thought to have caused accelerated genetic development and evolution and have also been responsible for the Ice Ages. It is possible that slight changes in the Earth's orbit allowed different gravitational pulls and radiation to emerge and that the ancients might even have known this. It seems that all or nearly all stone circles have an area of force within them which might be related to underground geological faults around 30 feet below the surface and also with hidden waters under pressure and what Guy Underwood in *Patterns of the Past* called 'Blind springs', centres where water rises vertically as in a natural pipe but when breaking through to the surface is forced to radiate outwards horizontally in one or more underground streams. Movement of waters through a tunnel of earth, particularly in clay, creates a small static electrical field. There is constant presence of magnetic underground water currents at the centre of earthworks and circles. Stones that are placed above streams that cross each other come to act as amplifiers for these energies.

Underground streams radiate out from the centre and the sacred places are linked by labyrinthine underground water currents. According to Underwood the blind springs create Spiral energy patterns and when the power emerges from the ground and up the stone it manifests itself in the form of a Spiral ascending around it in seven coils, the lowest two below the ground. This force or energy - totally unrecognised by science and physics by the way - waxes and wanes and changes polarity each month with the Moon. This Earth-force, Spirit of the wandering Underground Waters (Dragon/Serpent), has always been known to animals, plants and insects. Animals, birds and fish migrate guided by it and animal mothers seek out and give birth above its healing/holy Spiral 'blind springs'. Ancient peoples were natural dowsers and were also in tune with its energies. Dowsers respond as in a trance to the eletro-magnetism of the waters. To ancient women its waxing and waning according to the Lunar cycles and the Moon's gravitational pull on the tides would have been wholly natural. After all our menstrual cycles also wax and wane with the Moon, and the Moon rules the waters within our own bodies (in both women and men) and the birthgiving waters in our

60

wombs. It is only patriarchal men who find these mysteries difficult to comprehend!

Quartz in white crystal form is a constituent of every 'active stone'. The molecular structure of quartz is Spiral and may be left or right-handed as in the carvings at New Grange. If placed under pressure, as it would be if charged while inside another stone, alternate edges of its prism give off positive and negative voltages on quite a large scale. Perhaps it can also amplify forces other than electricity? The same forces that activated the stones also linked them and the direction could be left- or right-handed and usually changed monthly with the Moon. Hills and natural rock formations were linked into the network and the power was concentrated by human-made earthworks, stone circles and standing stones. Natural magic was released from the Earth's surface.

It is now known that women already in the Paleolithic era, as far back as 25,000 b.c., were beginning to work out the rudiments of a Lunar calendar by marking out the menstrual months on animal bones. These were during Neolithic times replaced by the more permanent record of circles of stones arranged in the form of a calendar for all to use and presided over by the Lunar and Great Waters Mother.

As the Moon waned, the polarity of the Spiral force altered, and the study of the Moon's orbit was absolutely essential. The Stones and the electromagnetic Spiral Force are everywhere associated with power, treasure, healing, life giving forces, fertility, sanctity, immortality, with giants, fairies, dragons, spirits and the Dead, the Otherworld, visions, trance-states and oracular powers, and now also with UFOs. They have the capacity to produce visions, 'supernatural' sensations, and generate life, and the 'treasure' is possibly the forgotten knowledge of how to increase the fertility of the crops. There are stories of cattle and crops dying if megaliths are interfered with or removed; there are tales of men crushed to death by stones when attempting to move them for the wrong reasons. It is possible that the Stones were used also for telepathic communication over vast distances. Our own human bodies are at one with and receivers for the magnetic waves given out by the unknown and undetectable (at least by 'scientific', 'analytic' and linear patriarchal methods) waves or emanations of the Dragon/Serpent, a force like warmth, running water or wind, that can be felt on the body. When women embraced the Stones they felt the Spiral energy flowing through their bodies. Is it possible that during the Lunar eclipses the collectives of women were in some way particularly open to Her energies and at their most powerful?

I have often experienced myself while menstruating and at times of the Full Moon being charged with pulsating and vibrating electric energies and greatly increased sexual powers as if every cell in my body were responding to Her greater energy. Our sexual energies are also of a waning and waxing, a spiralling nature. I have experienced being drawn up to the Moon while dancing ecstatically with a group of women.

It is a Spiral Force which gives birth to the Universe itself. The Milky Way is shaped in a spirally rotating wave pattern from which new stars are born. The DNA molecule that shapes life is a twin spiral. The Spiral and the Circle - primaeval symbols for the Great Cosmic Mother - ARE Life Energy itself (Mana), Cosmic Energy and Life Rhythm. She is the 'orgone energy' that Wilhelm Reich talked of!

The most universal legend is that of the power of the Serpent/Dragon, the magic powers of Water. She dwells in rivers and seas, in pools and wells, in the clouds above the mountain peaks, in caves and underground caverns; She regulates the tides, the menstrual flow, the rainfall and the thunder and lightning. Her energies are mostly beneficial, but they embody powers for both 'good' or 'ill'. To the christians, however, she came to represent the 'devil' and women and men who still communicated with and were consciously in tune with Her energies were vilified as witches and said to be in league with evil powers. Her Barrows, Stone Circles and Mounds have been found as far apart as Arabia, Africa, Tibet, China, India and North America, for example the famous Great Serpent mound at Ohio which is thought to date from the 1st century b.c.

Avebury/Silbury was THE most important sacred centre of all here in the North of Europe and would in ancient times have been connected with centres as far apart as Callanish in the Scottish Hebrides and Carnac. I find it interesting that it was my powerful experience at Avebury/Silbury that set me on my pilgrimage to reach Her other sacred centres. I visited Carnac the very next summer and in the summer of 1982 I made the long journey to Callanish on the desolate islands of the Outer Hebrides off the North-West coast of Scotland.

62

TREADING THE MAZE AT GLASTONBURY TOR

From St. Michael's Mount at Land's End in Kernow/Cornwall there runs a 200-mile 'Dragon path' through Glastonbury and Avebury. It goes through clusters of stone circles on the heights of Dartmoor and Bodmin Moor and there are a powerful collection of Dragon images in local churches dedicated to St. Michael and in folklore all along the path. In Avebury church itself there is a famous carving on the font of a bishop killing a Dragon. The early christians took over the Pagan places of worship, healing and ritual. On many of Her high places there are churches dedicated to Michael and dolmens and standing stones are even included in many of these well-nigh inaccessible churches perched as they are on high hilltops. Mont St. Michael is, as we saw, linked with the stone alignments at Carnac. It is a huge human-made mound. There is a Mont St. Michael as well off the coast of Normandy. On many of these flat-topped mounds there originally stood stone circles. These hills with artificially flattened tops and with coils of serpentlike earthworks encircling them and leading to the summits were known as Dragon Hills. It appears that the ancients danced the Serpent paths in procession to the summit in the same way that they danced the serpentine stone avenues that led into the stone circles.

Did the Mound contain a hidden treasure/power which could bring riches to the surrounding countryside? According to Michael Dames in his 'Silbury Treasure' the entire Neolithic population at Avebury gathered in the moonlight on Lammas night (August 1st) to witness the Pregnant Womb giving birth to the Harvest Child in interplay with the Moon and the waters surrounding the Mound. On the Dragon hills the Beltane fires were lit on the night before the 1st of May and the ancients used to roll fiery discs of straw down the hills, and torchlight processions descended from them to cleanse and fertilise the cattle and crops with Her magic and life-giving energies on the night to the Midsummer Solstice.

On May Eve/Beltane the sun rises at Glastonbury Tor exactly in line with Avebury forty miles away. The Tor was surrounded by marshes and isolated lake villages as late as 1000 b.c. It was worshipped by the Celts as the entrance to the Otherworld (Annwn) and was the sacred Isle of

Glastonbury Tor – with indwelling Goddess (1988). (Collection Alice Walker)

Avalon, the Isle of the Dead and of the Fairies, and the sacred World Mountain. It is the only known three-dimensional labyrinth, with its serpentine path winding to the summit in seven full circuits. There are rumours of there being a labyrinth also within the Tor itself and it is believed that King Arthur rests here, within the womb of the Goddess awaiting rebirth. It was also called 'The Island of Glass' and 'Caer Sidi', the spiral castle where the magic cauldron was housed. The Cauldron of Inspiration, later the 'Holy Grail' of Arthurian legend, belonged to the Goddess Ceridwen.

Glastonbury Tor is a natural hill that was formed and pushed 500 feet high by geological forces in ancient times. It has been shaped into terraces by human hands. Its original shape has also been altered so as to create mind-bending perspectives and visual experiences of being out of space and time. This it has in common with other sacred places of the Goddess that were moulded and altered by the Neolithic peoples. Glastonbury Tor has been terraced in the form of a labyrinth and the seven paths on both sides of the Tor were once walked for ritual and magical purposes by the entire farming community.

It is likely that the ancient peoples buried their dead on the Tor, it being a dry area in otherwise marshy land. In Celtic lore Avalon was the meeting place of the Dead, where people passed over into another existence. It is also thought to be surrounded by a vast zodiac engraved within the landscape and is called by some 'The Temple of the Stars'. By its foot lies a sacred well, Chalice Well, and nearby is the ancient city of Glastonbury itself. The Celtic fort which stands some distance away is called Cadbury Castle and is reputed to be the castle of Arthur's Camelot.

The journey through the maze or labyrinth, cut out in rock, turfcut as in Britain, laid out in stones as in Finland, or included in the design of entire temples or palaces as on Crete, was everywhere central to Her worship, the regeneration of the soul and of all of Nature. To cross over the paths, to get quickly to the summit, is dangerous and wrong. Here is my personal experience of a labyrinthine journey on Glastonbury Tor.[28]

On May Day Eve - Taurus Full Moon - 1980 a group of us set out to walk the maze of the Tor. It was led by Geoffrey Ashe, Kathy Jones (a Feminist psychic healer) and members of the local Glastonbury Matriarchy Study Group who had taken the initiative and organised the walk. Geoffrey Ashe[29] had, after many years of living close to the base of the Tor, finally walked the maze in its entirety and managed to make a coherent plan of its winding paths. He now had a vision of groups of like-minded people re-treading the maze and thereby recreating the ritual of the Neolithic peoples after thousands of years of neglect of the Earth's powers. May Day is one of the ancient festivals of the Goddess - and in Sweden at least, bonfires are lit everywhere on this date. This is how I experienced the night:

> Walking in torchlight procession - or at least attempting to do so - we arrived half an hour too late and couldn't at first find the others. We started walking in what seemed to us the direction that felt good...seeing the Moon, darkness, damp grass, slippery slopes, having difficulty in walking with our feet all the time at an odd angle...The paths not very clear after thousands of years of neglect, cows and sheep being the only creatures to wander and stumble to the summit. Time and again in the past I have found cows congregating on top of the Tor, their calm heads and horns outlined against the sky. Cow shit everywhere.

Although the Tor is always represented as a cone surmounted by the phallic remains of an ancient church (dedicated to St Michael, the Dragon-slayer) it is in fact shaped as a vast elongated humped Dragon which increasingly rises from hump to hump...Or as a recumbent female figure with the Tor forming its breast. Each terraced spiral is vast in its length...It takes some time to find the others and the torches, although we see the dark figures scrambling up and down the slopes in various places. One of my friends is menstruating, feels tired, has backache. We have to rest with her from time to time. We join the procession only to find it walking back the way we originally came from, slowly winding our way up and up. I feel though: who are most of these strangers, women and men, walking here with me? What have we in common? As most of us have never met before, don't know each other's intentions, how can we possibly experience and enact an ancient mystery? No way can we act collectively as one body, one mind, as is necessary to reawaken the ancient power; no way...

The Labyrinth is not fully walked by most of us, and when everyone finally gathers on the summit there is only an aimless wandering about, exhaustion, trying to shelter from the increasingly furious wind. A friend of mine has brought a chisel and a hammer with the intention of carving a women's symbol on the offensive, patriarchal tower that still stands there as a reminder of the Goddess-destroying male godhead. She is interrupted and threatened by a man who claims she is disfiguring a national monument. Feeble attempt at making a bonfire... We had not been given permission to do so by the National Trust who 'own' the land. On the tower there is carved, though, an image of Brigid milking a cow...

The original plan had been for all of us to spend the night on the Tor, by a bonfire, and then walk the maze down again at dawn. As it worked out most people went off after a while, feeling cold and vaguely frustrated, feeling the lack of some form of celebration or ritual that the long walk seemed to have been leading up to. Someone even suggested that what followed was in fact some form of punishment for unleashing powers that we are not able to channel or give form to.

Only a few of us remained on the Tor; four women and two men. We huddled closely together in our sleeping bags, and got some shelter from the wind at the foot of the tower. Everything was now in total darkness. I could, after a while, hear snores around me, but I was unable to get to sleep myself. Found myself trying to hang on to our covers with fists and teeth...heard strange sounds like rumblings and bells in the distance. This is a place of high magic, and this was a powerful night of the year. I seemed to be waiting for something: weird fantasies of UFOs arriving (and I'm in no way prone to this particular fantasy otherwise) - of enormous giants coming climbing across the Tor. All sounds are magnified up here, and so is climatic change; the Tor is utterly exposed, unprotected and naked. Through my closed eyes I seemed to see strange lights, and when I looked up I discovered the most wild and amazing lightning constantly criss-crossing the sky. All the years I've been in Britain I have never seen anything like this.

Some of the others also woke up now and someone said that she had heard stories of the lightning having been seen to strike the tower and spiral its way down to its base. We thought we might get fried alive if we remained where we were, so we scrambled out of our sleeping bags, stumbling half-awake away from the tower. Slithered, ran and fell the very long humpy road down the Dragon's backside, while all the while all along every few seconds we were as if in broad daylight while the next moment in total darkness: on - off - on - off... Figures illuminated against the sky...weird visual experiences. Total light but absolutely no sense of colour, like a photographic negative/positive. This added to our sense of fantastic unreality... Was this the Kundalini energy of the Tor awakened by our unfinished spiral walk? We had a feeling of being actively driven off the Tor. It was now about three o'clock in the morning. When we arrived at Her base torrential rain came down. (The strange thing is that I was writing this account late one night and the very next morning a letter arrived from Geoffrey Ashe in which he said, "Yes, I heard of the storm on the Tor after the maze-treading. A demonstration by the thunder god who is said to be the Goddess's arch enemy..." Was this a coincidence?)

We drove away, all of us wet and cold, cramped into the one available car. We arrived to a warm flat, with a fire and hot tea and food. Somehow we all felt an amazing energy despite it all, as if we had been storing the discharged energy or electricity of the storm within our bodies and psyches. At dawn a few of us drove back again to the Tor. We climbed up yet again, but this time taking the shortest path. The sun was not visible, and this time we found ourselves pelted by a hailstorm! Yet again we fled down the slopes and arrived back at the flat absolutely soaked to the skin.

The strange thing about this night was not only the wild storm, but also what happened to some of us in the weeks following; the profound effect it seemed to have on us. One of the women went back home and had far-reaching discussions with her husband about their life together. Another woman, a Lesbian Feminist who lives in Glastonbury and therefore is close to its power, found a few days later that while meditating she went into a trance that lasted many hours. She was unable to move or bring herself out of it. This had never happened to her before.

I myself found that I kept seeing images of the out-of-time-and-space distortions of the Tor that can clearly be seen and felt at certain points on Her humps. I am convinced that the ancients made these alterations to the mound deliberately so as to remove one into an experience of the Otherworld - not being able to locate oneself in space, to give one a feeling of the fantastic and the Other Reality; strange energies being summoned up in the landscape.

St Michael, the archangel of the christians, to whom so many churches are dedicated, was described in the 'Book of Revelation' as the leader of the band of angels who went to war against the Dragon ('Satan') and Her/his demon cohorts, and like St George was the successor to Wotan, the patriarchal Germanic slayer of Dragons. He was a kind of sun-god in fact, a 'heroic' patriarchal slayer of the ancient Mother, and pre-christian Glastonbury was a very important Goddess- and Underworld sanctuary that had to be conquered and suppressed. The Goddess was the Mistress of the Labyrinth of the Tor, as She was of Crete and amongst the Hopis.

Almost everywhere in the early churches one finds these images of St Michael or St George slaying the Dragon. The Serpent of Paradise is shown in old stained-glass windows as having a woman's head and breasts, and the Virgin Herself is shown crushing the Serpent's head under her feet. John Michell says that the church used this Dragon symbolism to represent the ancient power which is contained in ley lines, wells and megalithic monuments, and that the monuments, which were focal centres of local customs magic were in this way assimilated and consecrated by the early missionaries.

Not far from Avebury there lies a famous Dragon hill at the foot of the 'White Horse', a gigantic figure, 365 feet from nose to tail, cut out of the turf to expose the design in the white chalk underneath, at Uffington. Epona was the White Horse Goddess of the chalklands in the south-west of England and this is not the only place where one finds Her image on a rolling hillside. It has been debated whether the image, which can only be seen properly from the air and has the same kind of eerie feeling of being out of space and time and having strange energies and dimensions, is in fact that of a Dragon or a horse. Guy Underwood comes up with the amazing conclusion that the turfcut figure is indeed more that of a Dragon, but that the underlying water formations create the form of a horse! There are again some very strange and eerie energies at work in this place and as at Glastonbury Tor I get the distinct sense of being out of time and space. On the flat topped Dragon hill there are some barren chalk patches. It is said that the Dragon was slain here and that the patches are the place where some drops of Her blood touched the ground. As a result nothing will grow there, and so it seems...

LUNAR CONSCIOUSNESS

The ancients knew that there is a source of psychic sacred energy in the Universe which must also be renewed as it is drawn upon, that there is an interdependence of all things and a transmutation of one substance into another. They believed that the trees and stones absorb psychic energy from human emotion - and we now know that plants do also - and human rituals are necessary to fully activate the stone circles, that they are given, invested with, sacred power through the force of human worship.

Francis Hitchings tells of visions that Yorkshire artist Monica English has had within stone circles. She says that there was dancing and feasting within them for three days at each of the four major festivals of the year with processional movements, sacred fires, chants and music during which human emotion was poured out making the circles powerful. She says that the high point was the entrance of the Goddess Queen into the circle and the enormous reverence given her. The circle protected Her and also allowed the Life Force to enter Her. All the rituals led up to the great moment when she was possessed and made Her oracular announcements concerning healing, the safety of cattle and humans, future and past events. This was the original and natural 'witchcraft'.

In spite of writing this, Hitchings and other 'New Age' thinkers like John Michell, Martin Brennan and the 'ley hunters' and Findhorn people blandly keep talking about Megalithic 'man' and 'he', as if Neolithic culture was the creation of males. This usage of language is not only thoroughly sexist and patriarchal, it is also elitist since it assumes that not whole peoples but one man, in the singular, has achieved everything throughout 'history' (truly his story'). Who on earth is this mythical man/he that all the male historians are talking about?

Along with this goes also the assumption that ancient peoples were obsessed with mathematics, straight lines and geometry for their own sake. I don't honestly think that ancient women were much interested in abstract intellectual games as are present-day scientists who would happily blow up this world if by this means they could solve some 'challenging theoretical question'.

I think that ancient women - and men - had totally other priorities, that their Lunar consciousness (right side of the brain, Moon hemisphere, 'Isis' side of the brain according to the Egyptians) was very much open and alive and in no way dominated by the left (analytical, life-stultifying, linear, drily and rigidly intellectual) side of the brain.[30] It is with the psychic, trance-inducing powers of the Lunar mind that we are able to sense and absorb the Spiral energies of the stones and waters. The ancients believed that mind and mental powers were the gift of the Lunar Mother and that should She disappear all mental activities would cease. Mental powers and menstrual powers were seen as interrelated. It is only women who are capable of the heightened and intense emotional and sexual energies needed to activate the magnetic energies of the stones. These are precisely the qualities in women that men in patriarchy fear and that they set out to destroy. The church and the inquisition during the 'Burning Times' /Witch Hunts attempted to outlaw the Lunar consciousness in women as well as in those men who still saw themselves as the beloved sons of the Mother. Throughout all ages it tended to be the women who were mediums, oracles and psychics.

Ancient women and men were bisexual and not split apart within themselves. In patriarchies vast amounts of energy are taken up with suppressing our own and each other's bisexuality, in men policing women and ripping us off, and infinite amounts of energy go into acting out heterosexual gender roles. The ancient peoples were able to let their energies flow freely and were therefore able to gain great knowledge and psychic powers. Their knowledge was never gained at the cost of violating the Earth, or themselves, and was therefore life-enhancing. The exact opposite is true in all patriarchies where so-called scientific knowledge is gained at the cost of the utmost violation by men of our Lunar minds and the living being of the Earth. One-sided and unmitigated left-side brain knowledge ultimately leads to nothing but death and destruction.

There is much speculation concerning the magical and practical results of the power of the stones and the waters, and of the human communities interacting with each other. There is an old folk belief that if anybody places an object on the capstone of a cromlech and walks three times round it on the night of the Full Moon that it disappears. Psychics have felt the stones moving and dancing about in a circular direction, perhaps picking up the energies still remaining in the stones from the ecstatic circular dances that were once performed there. Perhaps people tapped out telepathic messages through them that then vibrated to other circles

70

across the land. Maybe levitation was possible along the energy lines and in this way the enormous stones could be teleported vast distances. Apparently there is a heavy sacred boulder in the village of Shivapur near Poona in India that levitates to shoulder level when eleven people (and it seems that any eleven people will do) dance around it and sing a certain mantra! It seems that so-called UFOs have mainly been sighted along these energy paths just as were the Dragons of old.

The Moon lives in the innermost watery recesses and caverns of our own bodies: we are of the same substance as both the Earth and the Moon. To Australian 'Aborigines' Spirals - which are closely connected with the Moon - represent sacred springs from which spirits can travel to and from the Underworld. Their sacred 'Chirunga Stones' were thought to contain the spirits of their ancestors. Native Americans treasured and were 're-charged' by their sacred 'Medicine Stones'. Holy wells and some stones, drunk of or touched or embraced - especially on certain days of the year - were seen to heal and prolong life. Natural crevices, caverns and caves - the vulva and womb of the Goddess – were powerful spirit realms and givers of immortality, healing and rebirth. Peoples living under patriarchy have lost the abilities to absorb these powers due to suppression of the Lunar mind and patriarchal science knows of no curative properties of stones and little enough of the healing mineral waters of the holy wells.

LIVING IN WALES

Where I live in Cymru/Wales near the west Pembrokeshire coast four
miles from the little town of Abergwaun/Fishguard in the province of
Dyfed, there were in the past strong links with both Ireland and Brittany.
This whole area has also a very strong Fairy tradition and it seems that
many UFO sightings have been made here. The cromlech near Trevine,
six miles from our cottage and lying by the sea, that I talked about before,
is known for its magic and Fairy legends. Some of the rock formations
along our Pembrokeshire coast are composed of the purple-pink
Cambrian sedimentary rock which is 7-8 million years old and is amongst
the earliest rock known in the world. It is precisely here that plans are
now being made for the dumping of nuclear waste from nuclear power
plants that are being shut down!

Everywhere there are caves in the rock looking like gigantic vaginas. Just
five minutes walk from the cottage where I live, which by the way is
called Dûr Bach, which means 'Little Water' or 'Little Stream' in Welsh,
there is a circular earthwork in a farmer's field. It feels like a vast circular
dance-floor, peaceful and meditative. I often go up there to centre myself;
we go up there on Full Moon nights to communicate with the Goddess,

The Pentre Ifan Cromlech near Nevern in north Pembrokeshire about
thirteen miles from us, was taken over as a place of initiation by the
Druids. In the oak groves nearby there was a school for neophytes. The
cromlech itself - which was called 'The Womb of Cerridwen' - was then
completely enclosed and formed a dark chamber within which novices
stayed for a number of days during initiations. Nevern, in the valley
below about three miles from the hilltop cromlech, is steeped in Fairy
lore and legends about the Tylwyth Teg, the Brythonic Fairy folk. In the
graveyard of Nevern church of St Brynach there stands one of the finest
Celtic crosses to be found anywhere. It is about thirteen feet high, has a
golden glow and is carved in fine, typically Celtic eternity knots. In the
church there is the Maglocumus Stone, dating back to the 5th Century
a.d., which is carved with the secret Druidic Tree-Ogham alphabet. Both
the church and the graveyard have an extremely ancient and eerie feel
about them and have reputedly been the setting for ghost lights and
phantom funerals in the middle of the night. One approaches the church

Cromlech Goddess 1982. (Inspired by Carreg Samson in West Wales)

through a tunnel of yew trees that appear to be extremely ancient and underneath which there is eternal darkness. Incredibly enough it seems as if yews can live for as long as 2000 - some say 3000 - years. These powerful trees were sacred to the Goddess and it is their presence here which gave a sanctity to the site long before christian times. It also appears as if the Yggrasil, the World Tree of Nordic mythology, was watered by a holy well, guarded by the Norns/Triple Goddess, and according to some accounts it too was a yew tree.

One of the yews is known as the 'Bleeding Yew of Nevern' and is apparently revered by Gypsies up and down Britain. As one walks through this tunnel of darkness one suddenly comes across the magnificent and glowing finely shaped Celtic cross at the side of the little church. It is very magic indeed. Many of the tales of Welsh folklore - *the Mabinogion* - first written down about 1200 a.d., have this setting as their background. Sometimes they have Sheela-na-Gig type female figures and faces and stones with the Ogham alphabet carved on one edge and the Roman on the other. Not far away are the Preseli Mountains from where the Blue Stones were brought to Stonehenge. The Preselis are sacred mountains and the whole region must have been of special holiness to the Neolithic peoples. They abound with stone circles, barrows, cairns, cromlechs and the remains of ancient habitations. The Bronze Age Great West Road that connected the south of England with Ireland went past here. The Blue Stones - spotted dolerites - were brought from Carn Menyn in the Preselis (Preselau Mynydd in Welsh) and they were apparently not quarried, but found on the surface, as the Bride Stones of Avebury are found on Wiltshire Plain; there are many still lying there on the mountain.

It is believed that up to ninety stones were brought to Salisbury Plain, the largest being thirteen feet long and weighing perhaps four tons. It is still a mystery how these stones were transported a distance of some 200 miles to Stonehenge around 1700 b.c. in the Bronze Age and why they were brought there. It seems probable that they had already been part of a much more ancient temple - of the Goddess - close to Carn Menyn where they originated. Gerald Gardner says in 'The Meaning of Witchcraft' that the Wicce believe that the inner horseshoe-shaped Blue Stone Circle represents the womb. It is horned and Lunar. The outer banks of Stonehenge are carbon dated to around 2700 b.c. and they are thought to have been completed - after being rebuilt many times - by 1600 b.c. The gigantic outer Sarsen Stones were 'erected' by the Bronze Age Beaker People, an aggressive and warlike tribe who had invaded Britain from the Continent. The earlier belief had been that unhewn stones were sacred (as seen at the more ancient Avebury) and that tooling desecrated them. The Sarsen Stones have been deliberately shaped.

The Witch legend of Stonehenge says that it is the Temple of the Great Goddess and symbolic of Her womb which the Druids called 'the Cauldron of Cerridwen' or 'the Cauldron of Inspiration'. Gardner says that the great occasion at Stonehenge was perhaps the Winter Solstice when the setting sun, on the day when it symbolically 'dies', appeared framed in the great trilithon over the altar. This trilithon represents the 'Door of the Netherworld', the Gateway through which the Sun passes at the Winter Solstice. The door or gateway was always the symbol of the

Great Mother from whom the new Sun was born[31]. Notice the striking similarity to the beliefs and practices at New Grange! It is also said that Stonehenge is aligned for the Midsummer Solstice sunrise and that the Druids believed that the sun-god Lugh/Apollo appeared there every nineteen years harping and dancing in the sky. This illustrates yet again how the later Druids, with their male solar orientation, diverted attention away from the much more ancient Lunar beliefs of the Mother. As I mentioned earlier 19 is a sacred Lunar number.

The Goddess promises rebirth from Her womb to humans as well as to the Sun. Gardner describes a Wicce celebration of Midwinter: the priestess stands behind the cauldron in which a fire burns while the coven's thirteen members dance around her sunwise with burning torches. This is called the 'Dance of the Wheel' or 'Yule'. Its purpose is "to cause the Sun to be reborn". The cauldron is the Gate of the Mother and the fire is the Sun-child in Her womb. In my mother tongue, Swedish, the word for Christmas is in fact 'Jul', which is almost the same word as that for wheel, which is 'hjul'. In Sweden we also celebrate the Festival of the Queen of Light or Lucia/Lucinda on the 13th of December. The Goddess is enacted by young women with long blonde hair who are dressed in long white gowns and carry crowns of living lights in their hair while it is still dark in the early hours of the morning.

Since writing my account of the Pentre Ifan cromlech and Nevern, I spent a truly magic day (March 9th 1983) visiting the cromlech for the first time. I had visited Nevern on a stormy autumn day more than a year before and the Celtic cross of the graveyard had inspired one of my paintings that later travelled in the 'Woman-Magic' exhibition around Europe. My friend Valerie Remy and I set out on a mild early spring day and hitched on the beautiful coastal road towards Cardigan, the ancient 'Bay of Rhiannon', to where a smaller road branches off on one side up to the cromlech and on the other side down to Nevern, which lies in a valley by a river. It turned into a day when nothing could go wrong and we felt as if guided all the way. We walked the three-mile long lane and paths leading to the cromlech and found ourselves by 'mistake' taking the 'wrong' path, one leading to the farm of Pentre Ifan. We both became convinced that this was an ancient Fairy path snaking its way through the forest and here and there crossing a winding serpentine stream. The atmosphere was such that we both felt as if 'stoned' and our hands tingled as if from hidden energies. The mood became meditative and trance-like. We had, however, to return down the path so as to find the road to the cromlech which is placed on high with a view of the Preseli Mountains beyond and the sea below. I later learned that 'Pentre' means village and that there was formerly an ancient settlement where the farm now stands.

This cromlech is different from any other I have seen: it is not at all making an enclosed shape, but on the contrary gives the distinct impression of being a 'gateway' to the earth mound that no longer exists. One can see the traces of the large oblong mound - the 'Womb of Cerridwen' - and it must have been truly impressive when it stood there in all its glory. Through the high 'gateway' one can see the mountain-top beyond. The capstone of the cromlech gives the impression of floating in space. It is so finely balanced on the tips of the supporting stones. A few stones still remain of the original enclosing Lunar/horned entrance to the mound.

Again one is struck by the extraordinary mushroom shape of so many cromlechs. I had not realised just how close this cromlech is to the sacred Preseli Mountains. Surely it is not coincidence that the Blue Stone inner Lunar horseshoe-shaped circle at Stonehenge is also called 'the Womb of Cerridwen' by the Wicce. It would appear that the ancient stone circles on the Preselis from where the Blue Stones were removed to Stonehenge were the Temples of Cerridwen, the Lunar Queen, and that this cromlech was a vital part of a vast network of sanctuaries on the mountains. Was this another New Grange, a temple within which the Moon and the Sun were seen to die and be reborn, Her miraculous womb of immortality and regeneration, abode of the 'living Dead', of the Spirit-Fairies and of the Tomb Mother? Here I would like to introduce you to the prayer of the Wicce.

She says: Whenever you have need of anything,
once in the month, and better it be when the Moon is full,
then ye shall assemble in some secret place...
to thee I will teach things that are yet unknown.
And Ye Shall Be Free from All Slavery...
keep pure your highest ideals;
strive ever towards it.
Let Naught Stop You Nor Turn You Aside...
Mine is the cup of wine of life
and the Cauldron of Cerridwen...
I am the Mother of All Living,

and my love is poured out upon the Earth...
I am the beauty of the Green Earth...
and the White Moon among the Stars,
and the Mystery of the Waters,
And The Desire In The Heart Of Woman...
Before my face,
let thine innermost self be unfolded
in the raptures of the Infinite...
Know the Mystery,
that if that which thou seekest
thou findest not within thee,
thou will never find it without thee...
For behold
I Have Been With Thee From the Beginning.
And I await thee now.
Blessed Be.

The primal mysteries of all religions emerged from women's direct biological and psychic experiences in planting the seed, in growing the child, in making a pot. Water, like Fire, was sacred to the Moon Mother. Women were the ancient makers and keepers of fires. Blood is the physical counterpart of the mystical Life Force circling throughout the Cosmos, nourishing the Universe, sustaining its breath and manifesting itself. (In patriarchies the source of Life - female and of the Goddess - is defined and hated as the enemy of male life). Women's menstrual powers and blood are of the essence of the creative powers of the Mother and are at one with the magnetic and mystic serpentine and spiral underground waters. Women first discovered how to use and produce fire and with the use of water brought about the transmutation of clay into another substance: they were the ancient potters and the pots were conceived of as the 'womb of the Goddess'. Women brought about the transformation of wheat and corn into edible bread and through the use of fire they found ways of drying, cooking and preserving foods. Women's internal menstrual and sexual fires create life within the watery caverns of our bodies. Women were constantly bringing about transmutations; with blood, with water, and with fire[32].

St Nons' Well (1982)

Brigid was not only the Goddess of Fire and Water but also the Goddess of Smithcraft. It was women's discoveries of directed heat and their invention of ovens for baking bread and other foods, as well as kilns for firing pots, that led to the making of furnaces within which fire could reach temperatures high enough to melt metals.

Women's knowledge of herbs had made them the natural healers. Some herbs could also be used for inducing hypnotic states and producing trances and visions in religious rites. The hilltop fire rituals and torchlight processions, the mysteries of the wells and the menstrual life-giving waters, the birth of the sun child in the womb/cauldron of Cerridwen, the Lunar Mother as the giver and creatrix of all life and mental powers, these were the mysteries of transmutation brought about through the Dragon/Goddess powers in women. Women were the mediators of the Goddess and the creators of early cultures too.

After having spent some time at Pentre Ifan figuring out some of these miraculous connections we made our way down the hill, across the road and into the valley where the village of Nevern snuggles by the river of the same name. It was getting towards dusk by the time when we finally entered the graveyard which, within the embrace of the yew trees, is eternally dark even on a sunny day. This is truly the abode of the Death-Goddess. The place felt even more eerie and weird than I had remembered it. We thought that we would like to return here again at Full Moon bringing candles with us, and later in the summer we did in fact do so.

I again felt the wonder of finding the amber-glowing Celtic cross by the church wall. It is extraordinarily powerful and its carvings very delicate as well as, I must say, pretty barbaric-looking. We went searching for the Bleeding Yew Tree among the dark, gnarled, gigantic tree trunks... I had not seen the tree when I visited the graveyard before. But now, as I turned around one of the trunks...I found it!

I wasn't prepared for the impact of it and my reaction was one of amazement and wonder: my hair was standing on end. I had a chill up and down my spine, a split second feeling of unreality, as I saw the dark red, tacky, blood-like substance seeping out as from a cunt or a wound in the trunk of the tree...It was truly astonishing...!

On the later visit we were four women who went with candles at midnight on the full Moon (which was also the Summer Solstice) to communicate with the menstruating Yew Mother. We felt a wonderful maternal presence, of peace and of healing, as we sat meditating around Her trunk, our little candles burning in the darkness. We felt absolutely no fear at being there in the graveyard at the 'witching hour'.

It was said that from along the coast of Pembrokeshire where I live one can see enchanted islands in the Irish Sea, especially if one is standing on turf taken from the yard in front of St David's Cathedral. David, the patron saint of Wales, was born here around 462 a.d. and is famous (or infamous) for having upheld the doctrine of original sin' against the 'Pelasgian heresy' at the synod of Brefi. He is known to have been a great missionary and christian teacher, but the fact that he upheld this patriarchal and bitterly anti-women doctrine doesn't exactly endear him to me. Legend has it that David journeyed to Jerusalem and was consecrated bishop by Pope John III. Here at the place named after him was founded one of the most important centres of christianity in Britain from where the Irish religious teachers came and vent. Near St. David's was the port for travelling across the Irish Sea. St. Patrick, born in 373 a.d., came here to study: St. Brynach of Nevern, a friend of David's, and many Breton saints, also studied here. For centuries this was an important centre of pilgrimage. In 1124 the pope conceded that in view of the perilous nature of the journey to Rome that two pilgrimages "to seek David" should be equivalent to one to Rome "to seek the apostles".

I was surprised the first time I went to St. David's, twelve miles from where I live, which today is a rather small city and only comes alive in the summer with the influx of tourists from England, to find an enormous cathedral and bishop's palace there. They were built in a hollow so that they wouldn't be seen by the marauding Vikings from the sea. The cathedral was, however, sacked and looted many times in spite of this precaution. It seems that this area was known in the earliest times for its oracular holy well, and here, as in so many other places, it was the well that originally gave sanctity to the site. St Non's Well lies a mile to the south of St. David's, overlooking the bay which is also named after St. Non, one of the numerous bays forming the ten mile stretch of St. Bride's Bay along the west coast. The Bretons claim that St. Non, who was supposedly St. David's mother, was born in Brittany, and there are many wells and chapels there dedicated to Her. The Welsh say that St. Non went to Brittany shortly after the birth of St. David. She was the matron saint of Dirion, in Finistère, where she was said to have been born. There is a chapel and a well there dedicated to Her, the chapel containing Her tomb, which is one of the historic Breton monuments. It is also said that She lived in a cottage on the site of St. Non's chapel. In the early eighteenth century it was said of this well: "There is a fine Well...cover'd with a Stone roof, and inclo'd within a wall, with Benches to sit all around the Well. Some old simple people go still to visit this Saint at some particular times, especially upon St. Non's day (March 2nd) which they kept holy and offer Pins and Pebbles at this Well." In 1811 it was noted that the "fame this consecrated spring has obtained is incredible and still is resorted to for many complaints". At the side of the well was a place where pilgrims could place votive offerings. Today there is a catholic retreat by the well and a shrine to "our Blessed Lady".

According to legend St. Non gave birth to St. David during a great storm in the night alone on this wild coastline. When she went into labour, She sank down behind a stone which promptly split in half as She gripped it, and where the child was born the miraculous well sprang up out of the ground! In a nearby field are the ruins of a very ancient chapel - reputed to be the most ancient christian building in Wales - which is surrounded by standing stones on one of which is carved the equiarmed cross within the circle. It seems that locally this is called 'St. Non's Cross' and is also interestingly enough a Neolithic symbol of the Goddess as the centre within the four quarters of the earth. This, like so many ancient Goddess symbols, has sadly been stolen by the fascists who use it for their own destructive patriarchal purposes.

I couldn't understand why St. Non, who like St. Brigid might originally have been the Goddess reduced to being a saint by the christians, should have found Herself in this wild and lonely place when in the last stages of pregnancy. This is nowhere explained in the official literature. But if the Well was an ancient healing and birth spring dedicated to Bride/Brigid (and remember that this is within Bride's Bay by the Irish Sea) She would naturally have come here when due to give birth. The priestesses of the Goddess were also healers and midwives and the most ancient sacred places were the precincts where the women came to give birth above underground healing Blind Springs and by holy Wells.

Brigid/Bride was the Great Goddess of the Celts and most likely very ancient indeed. She was the Goddess of Fire, the Waters, Poetry, Smithcraft, Healing and Inspiration. Her Serpent/Dragon cult centre had been at Kildare in Ireland and the sanctuary there had probably been oracular like that of Delphi, with its sacred flame, healing waters and indwelling spirit.

The most ancient temple at Kildare was a wattle enclosure within which was kept the perpetual sacred flame tended by nineteen Lunar priestesses ('Virgins') and there was the oracular and healing birth-giving well. No man was allowed to enter within this precinct. Well worship is universal amongst early peoples and there are many myths of Dragons dwelling in them. The Spirit of the Waters has a serpentine flow as witnessed by the movement of rivers across the land. Sacred mushrooms have helped me to 'feel' and 'see' this living Spirit, as well as experience the Wind as a presence, or being, who can be benevolent or hostile. Rivers everywhere are named after the Goddess in Her many forms. Brigid was worshipped all over Europe under the names of Bride, Briginda, Brigidu and Brigantia, 'the High One'. The Sanskrit word 'Brhati' means 'the Exalted One'. She was the union of Fire and Water and was called 'Brigit of the Ashless Fire'. She was depicted as triple-one aspect concerned with healing, one with divination and prophesy, and one with fire and iron-making. Perhaps She is the union of a Celtic and Indo-European (and more male-identified) Goddess with the earlier threefold Ma or Matronae who presided over all sacred Wells and were invoked as the source of all life. We have seen the importance of fire for the workings of the Megalithic sacred places, of torchlight processions and Beltane fires on the high places like a network of psychic transmitters. 'Tan' is the Welsh for fire and is associated with St. Anne. Many of the hills where the beacon fires were lit were called St. Anne's hills.

There are many wells in Brittany famed for their healing and divinatory powers, and the most popular of them are dedicated to Our Lady and St. Anne (the Mother of Mary), who is the matron saint of Brittany.[33] She, in turn, is a derivation of Ana/Inanna, Universal Goddess of Cosmic Waters and Childbirth. So it may well be that Ana, Anna, Non, Inanna and Brigid are one and the same, and St. Non's Well is Her Holy Well of Childbirth and Healing. Remember that it was Inanna who gave birth to the Sun at the Midwinter Solstice. By coincidence my own first name, and that of my mother and grandmother, is Anna and my family name, Sjöö, means 'lake' in Swedish - and I was born close to the Midwinter Solstice.

I mention this because St. Non's Well has had for me the most wonderful and miraculous importance these past few years. Before moving to Wales I had heard of the power of Wells because I belong to a Goddess-Pagan group that calls itself 'Wood and Water' and bases itself around the newsletter of the same name. It is dedicated to restoring and venerating ancient sacred Wells. In christianity Wells are either co-opted by the church or allowed to fall into ruin and total disuse. The waters of the Wells are the substance of the Goddess and I feel that they are at the very centre of the Mystery. Since living near St. Non's Well, visiting Her as often as I can at different seasons and times of day and night and drinking of Her holy waters, I have felt my life deeply affected by Her living powers. I made one recent visit to Her by the light of a Full Moon, a few days before Bride's Day on the 1st of February 1983. I have often felt guided in my paintings and on my journeys by Her. I found to my surprise when looking at a number of my recent paintings that almost all of them were about new life and that now after many years images of foetuses and pregnancy have reappeared in my work. At first I thought that perhaps I had some secret desire to have another child, but this is simply not so, and I realised that it was the birth-giving powers of the Well that were affecting me in this way. The Well has many powers to do with women's age-old medicine and has also helped a friend of mine to abort. She received back the spirit of the unborn child!

Celebrating Ancient Celtic Wales/Cymru (1983)

Brigid is also the Goddess of Crops, Cattle and Vegetation, and appears as a White Cow. She is called upon by women in childbirth and by the sick, and was so beloved that her worship continued well into christian times when she lived on as St. Brigid.

St. Brigid of Kildare, who was seen as 'The Mary of the Gael' and Mother of Jesus, was the most popular saint in Ireland next to St. Patrick. Her eternal fire was still tended by nineteen nuns in the monastery enclosure from which men were excluded. The fire was said to leave no ashes,

83

miracles were performed here and it remained a centre of pilgrimage and healing. In 1220 a.d. however, the archbishop of Dublin decided that the fire cult was 'pagan' and it was extinguished. But after his death the nuns relit the fire only for it to be finally put out at the Reformation when the monastery was also shut down for good. St. Brigid was said to have been a 5th Century holy woman who performed healing miracles and was the Matron Saint of the Hearth, Home and Sacred Wells. She was said to have been born at sunrise on the 1st of February, which is Imbolc or ancient Bride's Day. She was also spoken of as a priest or bishop and this in a church that claimed to never ordain women. By the Druids She would have been seen as the living reincarnation of the Goddess.

Stained glass

THE CULT OF THE SACRED WATERS WAS NOT EASILY DEFEATED

The church also fought well-worshippers and forbade divination by trees and stones. Both King Canute in England and Charlemagne in Europe campaigned against the Pagan beliefs. The Second Council of Arles stated in 452 a.d.: "... if in the territory of the Bishop, infidels light torches, or venerate trees, fountains or stones, and he neglects to abolish this usage, he must know that he is guilty of sacrilege." In 640 a.d. it was decreed: "Let no Christian place lights at the temples, or the stones, or at fountains, or at trees, or enclosures, or at places where three ways meet...Let no-one presume to make lustrations, or to enchant herbs, or to make flocks pass through a hollow tree or an aperture in the earth; for by doing so they seem to consecrate themselves to the Devil." (In the Mediterranean world the christians had been cruelly persecuted by the 'Pagan Romans' and as a result in their eyes all the ancient gods were evil and 'of the Devil'. The same wasn't true in the Celtic world and therefore the transition there was far gentler and more tolerant.)

But when such beliefs could not be defeated or destroyed, there was placed an image of the 'Virgin' - Our Blessed Mother - or of some saint, in a sacred tree or grove, over a holy well or fountain, on the shore of a lake or a river. A transformation was made and the country folk beheld in the brilliant images new and more glorious dwelling places for the spirits which they had long venerated. The church slowly got the people accustomed to praying to the saints, at the sacred water places, instead of the Spirits residing there, and this is the reason for all the statues of saints placed in niches at so many wells and fountains. The people had believed that it was by passing under the waters of a well that the Sidh - the abode of the Spirits in the tumuli or bills - was reached. There were circular well shrines in Sardinia in Neolithic times where circular stone structures enclosed the well waters below.[34]

Just as the cult of the fountains and wells was absorbed by christianity, so was the worship of the sacred trees, i.e. 'Our Lady of the Oak' at Anjou. Sometimes a whole tree would be enshrined in the wall of a chapel in the same way that standing stones and whole cromlechs were included in some churches. There are haunting images of the 'Virgin' - often shown standing on a Lunar crescent - deep within grottoes, as at Lourdes where there is also a wonder-working well. Others are found far out to sea or high in the treetops. There were pilgrimages held to the fountain of St. Anne of d'Auray in the Morbihan, in Brittany, with a pardon lasting three days and with torchlight processions at night. At the time of the Eleusinian Mysteries in Greece the initiates had searched for Persephone by torchlight and had visited the seashore and the sacred well. In the same way sacred processions carried the image of St. Anne with the Mary child in the night and all-night services were held in the dimly lit church of St. Anne where special masses were held for the saints and the Dead. Offerings were given to the sacred pools and lakes; rivers in Europe were named after the Goddess, i.e. the Danube and the Donau (Danu of the Celts). In the druidical forest at Broceliande there was the Fountain of Baranton which was famous from the Breton legends of King Arthur, Merlin and Vivian. As late as 1835 the congregation went there, in a time of severe drought, and prayed for rain. There was also the Fountain of St Cornely at Carnac.

During May 1983 our 'Woman Magic' exhibition was shown in Cologne (Köln) and in Bonn in West Germany; in June it went to Dortmund. It was strange for me to find that the Women's Culture Centre/Bookshop where the exhibition was shown in Köln is called 'Rhiannon', strange considering that Rhiannon was the Mare Goddess of Wales. Indeed Cologne itself, now a catholic city, was once a great and important Celtic centre possessing an oracular well as a place of pilgrimage. Over this well the Romans built a temple of Dionysus and finally the christians constructed their enormous cathedral, the Dom, on this sacred site. Other ancient pre-Celtic and Celtic holy places all over Europe were taken over by the Romans and dedicated to Isis, the Dark Mother of the Egyptians. Much of Her ritual was later absorbed by the early catholic church and the temples of Isis were transformed into cathedrals dedicated to 'Our Lady', Queen of Heaven, Moon of the Church. I heard that the Rhine Valley was powerfully Matriarchal and that even in later times ships carrying images of Isis would travel down the river ablaze with living lights and torches. This use of living lights in the worship of the Holy Mother is today very prevalent in all catholic shrines of Mary.

In the Romano-Germanic museum, situated next to the Dom in Cologne, there are some very mysterious stone-carved images of the 'Matronae'; Triple Mothers of the Celts. The images are Roman but appear to portray actual Celtic priestesses in enormous-looking Lunar headdresses and wearing shawls fastened with a large brooch. They all wear Lunar necklaces. They make one think of the Three Norns of

Nordic mythology, or the Three Fates or Fairies. The Matronae are mature women of great dignity. They are seated and in their arms they hold bowls of fruit and other riches of the earth.

They must have been the original guardians of the oracular well. Similar shaman-priestesses would have dwelt by the hot springs and healing mineral waters of Aquae Sulis of Bath in Britain, and at many other sacred wells. Bob Stewart says in his book 'The Water of the Gap: The Mythology of Aquae Sulis' (1981) that Bath was an oracular Otherworld cult centre with a living Goddess myth-cycle, and that 'Sulis' means 'gap', 'eye', 'orifice' and 'whirlpool'. The cave-like structure from which the hot waters stream and hot vapours emerge was the Vagina, the Still Centre, Gateway to Her magical Otherworld. It was the transformative Cauldron of Cerridwen within which all life forms. As at Delphi in Greece, the priestesses would have been possessed by the Pythonic Spirit of the Chthonic Mother (Gaia) and would have entered into trances while breathing in hot steam from the Underworld while the Spirits of the Dead spoke through them.

The catholic church co-opted and took the credit for the healing powers of the wells. There are wells under the cathedrals at Nîmes and at Sangres. At York Minster I visited the crypt where the well is still to be seen, but unfortunately the 'guide' was a priest who felt it his duty to say a lord's prayer just to be on the safe side! The large and beautiful cathedrals of 'Our Lady/Notre Dame' in France are built over oracular wells, Chartres Cathedral stands on an ancient Neolithic mound within which was a grotto with a sacred well. This was a place of pilgrimage for the whole of the Celtic world. According to Anne Kent Rush[35] there was, within this grotto, an image of the Dark Mother, one of the oldest wooden sculptures of the Goddess to be found in Europe. It was carved in the hollowed-out trunk of a pear tree and showed Her giving birth - "'Virgin Paritura' about to give forth." She was the dark Goddess of the Underground Waters, of Death and Rebirth, also venerated by the christians who after hearing mass in the cathedral went to sing psalms to pay honour to 'Our Lady of Under-the Earth'. The pilgrims went from the mound by a passage leading to a crypt, to visit a grotto where the Black Virgin was to be seen; there they made their devotions and were sprinkled with holy water from a well. During the French revolution this sculpture was hauled out and ceremonially burnt!

There are other such ancient, probably pre-christian images of the Lady of the Underworld, Queen of Night, Dark of the Moon, in Europe. She is connected in folk tales to Her healing powers and Her love of water and the dark, and Her shrines are often in underground grottos close to water sources. One such wooden image of the Black Mother (La Vierga Negra) is to be found in the little town of Montserrat nestling high up in the Holy Goddess Mountain of the same name not far from Barcelona in Catalonia in Spain. She was found some hundreds of years ago in a grotto in the mountain by some shepherds and is the Goddess of the region. The Montserrat mountain is immense, whitish in colour with weird and fantastic rock formations which resemble strange gigantic women-beings in long skirts with hooded heads. Many rare herbs and plants grow there. On Her pinnacles there are many hermitages, but typically Her holy mountain has been co-opted by male monks.

I made a pilgrimage to her in the Winter of 1983/84. In May 1957 I happened 'by chance' to be present at the yearly Romany festival at Les Saintes Maries de la Mer, in the Camargue by the sea in the South of France. There Romanies come from all over Europe to worship their Dark Mother Sarah who dwells in a small crypt-like church, and to feast and sing, dance and trade. I remember the eerie feeling in the dark womblike church.

The cathedral of Notre Dame de Paris, which stands on the mandorla-shaped (vagina) island in the River Seine is also built where there was formerly a temple of Isis. I have experienced a real 'high' standing where one is bathed by the multifaceted blue light emanating from the three absolutely magnificent and magic, huge and circular stained glass windows.

Even into Medieval times there were very strong Craft traditions in the country around the Rhine. I was told that the two Dominican monks who wrote the infamous 'Malleus Maleficarum' (Witch-Hammer) in 1486 were based in Koblenz. This document, full of vitriolic sexual hatred of women, was the 'bible' of the witch-hunters and the Inquisition. During the 'Burning Times' in Germany some of the villages and towns of this countryside lost virtually their entire female population at the stake. I am glad to say that while staying in Köln I was able to visit a contemporary and thriving group of feminist Wicca who live and practise healing in the beautiful countryside not far from Koblenz. They are keeping the ancient women-traditions alive and well.

Ironically just north of Cologne lies the dreadful, polluted and heavily industrialised Ruhr. The smoke pouring from the innumerable chimneys around the coalmines and ironworks there helps to create the acid rain that is fast destroying lakes and forests as far away as Sweden and Finland. I had the opportunity to see something of the Ruhr since our exhibition next went to Dortmund in June 1983. While there I was taken to visit the Externsteine, near Paderborn, in the Teutoburg Forest. These most ancient rocks that are colossal and extraordinarily shaped were (or so it seems) the sacred centre of Germany and perhaps another World Mountain or Navel where different realities merge and can be entered. There appear to be gigantic heads, faces and figures carved all over the rocks and it is very difficult indeed to tell whether they are natural formations or forms altered by human hands. The legend tells that Sibyl, an oracular priestess, once lived in the cave/temple on one of the rock pinnacles and that no man was allowed to enter up there.

At a later time it was perhaps a Mithras temple and later still it was taken over by Dominican monks who seemed to have had knowledge of the ancient Dragon power-centres of the earth and tried to use and control the energies for their own political ends. This is also true for the Nazis who in recent times practised sun worship in these very rocks. It seems the Externsteine have had a long and strange history. I have also read that present-day German witches gather here in the rock-cut temple high up in the rocks to watch the sun at the summer solstice and to celebrate with rituals in the nearby forest. The Teutoburg Forest is where the Romans were defeated by the Germanic tribes and there are also healing and curative wells in the area.

HOLY WELLS IN DENMARK

I was asked by the Danish Women's High School to initiate or lead a course in 'Women Culture and Art' for two weeks in August 1983. The school is run by women for women, is economically supported by the Danish state and is situated near Tønder on the German border in Jutland. It was been going now for about five years and there have been courses there over the years in Matriarchy, dreams, healing and witchcraft as well as carpentry, farming and so on. Before going to the school I enquired whether there were any holy wells in the vicinity, but to my surprise no one knew anything of such wells. I wanted to include ritual work with a well as part of our course which was going to include exercises from Starhawk's book 'Dreaming the Dark.[36] We decided to go to the local library to see if we could find any books or information on the subject, and found that there is in fact such information still in some old rare books. We also found out that there is a holy well in a village only a few miles from the school and that the directions to find it were set out in detail.

So we set out - three women - on what we were to experience as a mystery journey, a pilgrimage, with powerful effects on us and other women. I had been going through a depression for a couple of months prior to this, but seeking for and finding the well turned my mood, healed me, and I became from then on much more positive and energetic.

He drove off to the little village and found the old white house with the garden in which the well was to be found. When knocking on the door we were told by the old man who answered it that we were to go and talk with his wife in another house nearby. He said "she knows all about the well. You go and talk to her". And so we did. Again we knocked on a door and an old and very dignified woman appeared. We said, a bit feebly, that we were interested in the Holy well, at which she looked us deep in the eyes and said, "I believe in its powers". When we said that we did too she relaxed, smiled and asked us in for a cup of coffee. Then she talked to us for hours, about her family, the history of the village and so on. She brought out a big old scrapbook in which she had collected a lifetime's information, both handwritten and newspaper cuttings. She finally told us that we could borrow the book for a couple of days to photocopy some very old newspaper cuttings telling the extraordinary story of the holy well. We felt very honoured that she treated us with this precious material and the women at the school were amazed and delighted when we brought it back. It was greatly admired and read. We found out that the well is simply called ' Helligkilden' (Holy Well) and that the old house was named after it. The white house and its garden have been in the old woman's family for 300 hundred years.

There were indeed many stories of miracle healings – of the blind who could now see again after visiting the well, of crutches thrown away by people who had once been disabled. Some of them went back to the eighteenth century. The waters of the well were known particularly for bringing down high fevers and the old lady said that there are still people today who sneak into the garden to drink of its waters, even though nowadays its mouth is covered with a heavy concrete lid. In the 1920s someone from the village thought of sending a bottle of well water to a lab in Copenhagen to be analysed. It was found to be radioactive. A company was formed to bottle the water on a large scale and send samples far and wide by train, even as far as Switzerland, and sell it at high prices. The first summer they made £5,000, but after a while the costs involved in transporting the bottled waters got too expensive, the family lost money, the men involved quarrelled and the well fell into disuse and was slowly virtually forgotten. We thought to ourselves that this economic failure and ruin happened because no way will She let Her Waters be exploited and used for the benefit of greedy men. By the way, in Scandinavian languages and in German the words for well (Källa, Kilde, Born, Quelle) are the same as for 'beginnings', 'origins', 'source' and 'birth'. In English well is also used in terms such as 'well-being', 'all is well', 'feeling well' and so on. Interesting.

We returned on the Saturday to the old woman to give her back her book, and yet again we listened to her talking for a long time, sitting in the old house surrounded by beautiful old furniture and long-cherished family possessions. Now at last we had proved our sincerity and genuineness to her and she allowed us to go to the well and fetch some of its waters back to the Women's High School. In the morning when leaving the school we had not been able to find a glass jar and so we had brought a large plastic container to collect the water in. It took us a while just to move the very heavy and large concrete lid inch by inch, but at last we had a clear crescent opening into the well and could see into the dark waters. Because the well had been built up and a pump put into it, the waters were far down and difficult to reach. Also they didn't look very clean at first, sight, but then I saw a frog in the water and knew that such creatures will only live in healthy waters.

We then had a difficult time trying to submerge the plastic container long enough, and out of reach, to fill it with water. At last we managed to fill it almost half full. Quite miraculously the opening that the lid and the well structure formed was that of a perfect large silvery crescent Moon reflected in the mysterious black waters below. We all felt that we were taking part in something very special and sacred. The view from the holy well was into the garden with its fine old trees and on the other side across fields into the far distance.

We proudly brought the waters back to the High School where they were eagerly awaited. Never before had there been a plastic container in the school fridge on which was said "Holy Water"! We found over the next week that just about every woman in the school went there to take a sip and to wash their aching limbs in it. Some of them experienced its healing powers. During the rituals we enacted as part of the 'Women culture' course I found myself identifying powerfully with the Dark Mother of the Underground Waters, of Life and Death. From some old books in the library in Tønder I pieced together the following account of wells and well worship as it was practised until fairly recently all over Europe by the common people.

During the summers in olden times (long before there were any fridges), when all the water from rivers and lakes was lukewarm to drink, it was only the clear and cold water from the wells that was refreshing and exhilarating - it made you feel 'high' and heady. I remember as a child my own delight when coming across and being able to drink the water from some cool clear well deep in the Swedish forest on a hot summer afternoon. A 'holy well' is one that is powerfully and miraculously healing at some certain time or times in the seasonal year. People would have noticed that animals came here to be healed and that the grass was greener and the earth more fertile in their vicinity. Some holy wells have also sprung up in particularly freaky and special places, like from an ancient mound, from within a hollow tree-trunk or on the sea shore.

In Scandinavia it was at Beltain and on Midsummer Eve (summer solstice) that the wells were magically powerful. In Sweden at Imbolc the snow still covers the ground and it is not until Easter and the beginning of May that the Goddess dips Her finger (throws a warm stone) into the waters and begins to warm them. Then Nerthus (Brigid of the Notherners) rides across the land in her solar wagon drawn by she-oxen as the new green life of Spring comes into bud. The Spring Festival was celebrated some time between April 21st and May 11th (not on a fixed date) when also the cows were let out to grass. Beltain is, in Scandinavia, called Valbergsmisse Eve and in Germany Walpurgisnacht. This was the night when the Wicca were believed to fly or ride to Blåkulla (in Sweden) and to Bloksbjoerg (in Denmark) - both of them mountains. Sacred fires, in Germany called Hexenfeuer or 'witches' fires' were lit on the high places to guide their way, or so the story goes. Valborg was Valuburg, an ancient Sibyl or Witch. Originally She was Nerthus, the Great Mother, and this is Her festival and Her season.

Nerthus was associated also with Urth, one of the Norns whose magical Well sustained the Yggdrasil or World Tree. May 1st was known as Rowan Witch Day and according to Merlin Stone (Ancient Mirrors of Womanhood', Vol. 11), "the tiny orange berries of the rowan were used to ease childbirth, which probably led to its alternative name of Quickbaum (life-tree)," When Nerthus/Niortha goes forth in the Springtime in her cow-drawn wagon with its solar Wheels from Her sacred grove on Sjoelland (the same Island on which Copenhagen was built and which She created) the days are blessed. No man went to war, all iron was locked away and no weapons were to be found on this day. Peace truly reigned. Fires were lit all along Her path and the well waters partook of Her powers. When She finally returned to Her sacred grove, Her wagon and Her image were washed by blindfolded slaves (we are only guessing that they were slaves), who were then strangled and drowned in the lake by Her priests. We must remember that this was already into the early Iron Age with its emerging patriarchal male priesthood, its warfare and slavery. Professor Glob writes about this in his book 'The Bog People'. Many of these human sacrifices have in recent years been found, extraordinarily well preserved, in the Danish peat bogs.

I'd like to point out here that although it is possible to find out a fair amount about the ancient Norse religion it is almost impossible to get information about the culture of the earlier, small and dark Sami and Finn peoples who were probably the original inhabitants of Scandinavia after the last Ice Age. As we saw earlier they might be related to the Neolithic peoples who created the stone circles and mounds in Britain. The Samis are a shamanistic and nomadic people who have been more or less written out of the official history books that are full of racist and

93

sexist assumptions. They are presently being driven further and further north as they are deprived of their traditional lands, sacred sites and culture. The history of the oppression of the Sami peoples is very similar to that of Native Americans and the Inuits/Eskimoes to whom they are related. They are now becoming more militant - as witness the struggle at Alta River where the Samis with supporters attempted to stop the building of a hydroelectric dam that would endanger the existence of the last surviving Sami community in the north of Norway.

'Earth is our Mother We must take care of Her' (1984)

To return to the wells, many fires were lit near them on Walpurgisnacht and rituals were performed there. Peoples everywhere believed in the cleansing, renewing and protective powers of the sacred fires and cattle were passed through the flames for protection and healing. The Midsummer Festival was, on the other hand, always on June 24th in Scandinavia and is still popular as perhaps the greatest feast day of the year, together with Yule at Midwinter. In Denmark Midsummer Eve is called St. Hans Eve after Join the Baptist, who supposedly was conveniently born on this day just six months before the supposed birth of Jesus at Midwinter. In many parts of the world this night is celebrated with sacred fires (in Germany called Johannisfeuer) and is famous for its well journeys. In Denmark alone there are 200 wells known to have been visited by great numbers of people on St. Hans Eve.

In Sweden all of Nature is in Her most wonderful bloom on Midsummer's Eve and the nights are light. Many plants are then in fruit and animals pregnant. Flowers and herbs that bloom then and early potatoes are named after St.Hans, and nine of these plants were collected and kept for protection. The early morning Midsummer dew had particular healing powers and if one treads in it barefoot one absorbs its powers and recovers life energies. The sick rolled around in the dewy grass and clothes were rinsed in dewy water to protect their owners from ill-health in the coming season. Dew was of the very essence of the Lunar light and life-giving Waters of the Mother.

The most famous and most visited of the Midsummer wells in the whole of Denmark was St. Helene Kilde (Well) at Tisvilde, in Odsherred on the seashore of North Sjaelland. Helene Kilde is situated on the seashore, the especially sacred place where sea and land meet and where sometimes the sea-waves caress the well. The sea gives us the precious salt and the ocean is the ancient Mother of all life. Associated with the holy well appears to be a strangely shaped stone that has the markings on it as from a recumbent woman's body. It is situated along with two other wells, also called after holy women, St. Karen and Tove, in a large cleft in the seashore hillside. Nearby is 'Helene's Grave' and the remains of an old well chapel, and three miles inland lies Tibirke ancient church. There are wells with similar legends attached to them and dedicated to women saints in Skåne in the south of Sweden.

There are many versions of the legend around these wells, one of which says that a holy woman called Lene was murdered in Sweden and that her dead body sailed across the sea on a stone. When her body reached the island of Sjaelland the hillside burst open to allow her to enter and where her body came to rest a well sprang forth. People tried to bury her in the nearby churchyard, but the body could neither be moved nor carried. So Her grave is here on the seashore, which in fact was seen as particularly protective of the Dead and where many ancient burials places are to be found. The drowned were always buried by the sea.

Another version of the legend has it that Helene, a Swedish princess, tried to avoid the clutches of a lovesick king by throwing herself in the sea. She was rescued by a stone that floated on the water and on it she sailed to Denmark. The well sprang forth where she set foot on land and she lived here as a holy woman for many years. Yet another version has it that three holy sisters wanted to sail across the sea but they died on the way and were brought by the waves to different places where wells burst forth. There appear to be a number of Helene 'Kilder' (wells) in Sweden and Denmark and they obviously must relate to the Goddess in Her Midsummer aspect. Is She the Helene of the ancient winding tracks that Guy Underwood talks of in his 'Patterns of the Past', the Earth Spirit that journeys across the landscape sanctifying wells, stones and mounds. It was said that when the sea is at its lowest ebb - on St. Hans Eve - a large stone becomes visible in its waters and on the stone there are the markings and a hollow as from the holy woman's body. The stone miraculously floats on the sea and brings the Goddess to Denmark's shore and where her feet tread healing/holy wells appear and the land becomes fertile.

It seems that in fact in ancient times Helene was called Helle-Lene and Hella was the Goddess of the Dead and possessed the transformative Cauldron of Birth and Death. Her land of the Spirits, the Fairies and the Dead was situated next to the roots of the World Tree, the Yew Yggdrasil. Yews can, I am told, live for as long as 3,000 years. They often grow in old sacred graveyards as at Nevern in Wales and are associated with the Dark Mother, but also with birth. Midwives traditionally carry a piece of yew wood for protection at birthings.

In Germany the Goddess was called Holle and Holda. She later became Queen of the Elves and Fairies and of the Witches. Her name also means 'holy', 'heal', 'hallow', 'hole' and 'whole', as well as 'all', 'halo' and 'holly'. In the Nordic sagas I learnt about as a child the Huldra was clearly both the Goddess of the Forest and the Animals and of Death. She was portrayed as a beautiful naked woman with long blonde hair, but Her backside was dead and hollow and She had a tail like an animal. (The sagas told that She lured lonely men to their deaths!) Perhaps originally Hella or Holle was a Goddess of these Wells? Helle-Lene was transformed into a christian saint, St. Lene, in medieval times. In Denmark as everywhere else holy wells were early taken over by the catholic church and given names of christian saints (like St. Hans). The church even built special well chapels to divert the people from the actual well and its in-dwelling spirit where they could pray to Maria, 'God's Holy Mother' for help or in thanksgiving. There were special prayers and psalms. Some of these chapels were later extended and became parish churches, but most of them fell into ruin. Many cloisters were built by the Wells.

In many countries even today there are still well chapels where people pray, hang up their crutches if cured after bathing in the well water, discard their old clothes as offerings and leave money in the troughs for the poor. The water from the wells was collected and kept all the year round as medicine.

From time immemorial until around 1900 the Danish people visited their holy Wells and the church could do nought to stop it. Here is an example from Ireland which could just as well be applied to Danish wells: "At the well of St. Declan, Ardmore, County Waterford, about a century ago masses of people assembled annually on December 22nd, crawled beneath a hollowed stone and then drank of the well. It was surmounted by the image of a female figure which is described as being "like the pictures of Callee, the Black Goddess of Hindostan." The catholic priests "actually whipped the folk away from the spot, but to no purpose" (Lewis Spence, 'Irish Goddess and Kali', 1948).

It is only finally with the takeover by modern male-dominated technological medicine from the ancient and primeval women's herbal knowledge - after the end of the Burning Times - that the healing powers of the Wells got forgotten and were denied. The vital fluid of our Earth Mother's body, her life-giving menstrual flow welling out from vulvas, gaps and clefts, Her magic cauldrons of Life and Death, are being polluted, destroyed and raped at our own cost and tragic loss of abundant and life-giving healing energies.

At many wells, far into medieval times there was still the ancient memory of the association with women's blood, but the blood they were now connected to in legend and myth was blood unwillingly given from the bodies of murdered women. It was now said at the many 'Maiden Wells' that the water had welled out of the ground where the blood from a murdered or raped virgin had fallen, or a woman killed by her husband or by robbers, or a mother who cried for her murdered children. One story goes that a woman was murdered by her husband because she had shown disrespect in church: she had burped during a sermon!

Another famous well in Denmark is named after Risia, or St. Regisse, who was said to have been beheaded within a sacred grove by the farmer she worked for. Other versions of the legend tell that she sank into the ground where the holy well now is. A church is built on the mound in which she lies buried.

A sacred pond or bog is supposed to have gained its healing powers from a white horse that is said to have drowned there. One remembers the British Horse Goddesses Epona and Rhiannon. I wonder if in fact and at some time in patriarchal history actual women were sacrificed to the holy wells by a male priesthood who were out of tune with the Goddess, had forgotten the meaning of Her waters and had co-opted and perverted the original rituals and functions of the well-priestesses so as to promote their own powers and male control.

St Helene Kilde and St Regisse Kilde were to be visited three years at a stretch and some holy wells were visited at three or four different feast days of the year. At these two very important holy wells sick people slept on the earth around the water, or on the holy woman's grave in the vicinity, during Midsummer night. It was believed that total healing would then be achieved and that the holiness of the ground itself was absorbed into the bodies of the people who were ill. The sick slept an incubatory sleep during which healing took place. This was always the way of the Goddess...

For the Midsummer Feast the wells were decked in flowers and garlands, in green finery. This custom is still alive in the small towns around Sheffield in England where at the end of June the whole church congregation follow the priest and the church choir in a round of well blessings. The most famous holy wells are in Tissington and beautiful vibrant images are created with entirely organic materials like flower petals, leaves, moss, wool and sand (although sadly of mainly biblical motifs) and raised above the wells. It is girls and women mostly who spend months making these short-lived images. When travelling to a holy well on St. Hans Eve one had to come in silence and not even greet friends. No bustle of noise was allowed however many people were waiting their turn by the Well, and if the peace was broken the waters disappeared and only returned when it was restored. The water was thought to be most powerful after sundown or at midnight.

Everything had to be ritually repeated three times. One walked three times round the Well or jumped over it three times, drank three mouthfuls or glasses of water, fetched the water for three Thursdays in a row, bowed three times to the rising Sun, bent three times over the well. The sick person walked three times round the well chapel and shouted her or his illness three times at its altar. Witches walked three times Moonwise around the Well to undo some magic.

The water was to be drunk for internal illnesses and used for washing for external ones. Old clothes were thrown away along with bandages and crutches. Many beggars came to the well markets to ask for the discarded clothes. The new clay mugs, bought in the market, were thought to now possess healing powers even when ordinary water was used in them. To be entirely effective as a cure the sick should revisit the Well nine days later and then again nine days after that. One should wash oneself in utter silence. If you drank from the waters of a holy well on Midsummer's Eve together with your beloved then you would soon be married to each other.

It was thought that droughts were caused by badly kept wells and that when a well was cleared it would rain. Catholics dip their holy cross in a well to bring rain. The farmers in Scandinavia continued the tradition until quite recently of honouring the Dead at the seasonal festivals and making sure that the peace of the Dead/Fairies was preserved and protected within the mounds. On the festival nights a bowl of porridge or an offering of milk was brought to the burial mound that shared the name with the farm nearby. The milk was for the serpents who represented the spirits of the Dead and were totem animals not to be harmed. It was thought that without the milk the serpents would not successfully shed their skin to renew themselves.

The Dead and the Serpents are of the nature of the Dark Mother of the winding Underground Waters, the sacred Stones and Mounds. As the Serpent sheds its skin and is reborn anew so the Moon eternally waxes and wanes but never dies and women shed our womb lining in our monthly menstrual flow. We bleed, but we live and we create life: we are of the nature of the Goddess of the Holy Wells.[37]

SOLAR MADNESS: BARRENNESS IS A PATRIARCHAL CONDITION

The alchemists of medieval times sought the philosopher's stone and the elixir of life, the secrets of the transmutation of base metals into gold, of spiritual transformation, the quest for immortality and for the holy grail - the wonder-working vessel that was originally the Cauldron of Cerridwen. I wonder whether the mysterious womb-caverns where the Dragon guarded the treasure and the miracle-working life-giving Wells were not the original and natural 'grails' long before cauldrons were forged by the Iron Age Celts. And before the cauldrons there were the clay pots made by women and experienced by them as the transformative womb of the Mother and 'decorated' with Her Spirals, Breasts and ever-staring Eyes.

Brian Easlea,[38] a former physicist who opted out in the 1960s when he perceived that present-day scientists were trying to unleash the terrible destructive forces of the sun god, has traced the progression through the ideas of patriarchal philosophers from the Earth being seen as life-giving Mother, to Her vilification and desacralisation as a wilful Mistress who desires to be subdued by a masterful lover, to a young Virgin daughter raped by her father, and finally to being nothing but a machine of dead matter. According to these patriarchal philosophers it is only thanks to the heavenly solar father that she and all living beings are endowed with the spirit of life.

Easlea traces what he calls 'patriarchy's confrontation with woman and Nature' back to Francis Bacon, the founding 'father' of the new science whose efforts led to the establishment in the 1660s of the first science academies which coincided with 'victory' over the witches. Before the new male philosophy and the coming of modern medicine with its all-male priesthood of doctors[39] could take over, the ancient women's cultures, knowledge and religion had to be wiped out finally once and for all: the Pagans ('People of the Land') and the Heathens ('People of the Heath') among the peasants had to be defeated.

Bacon, like Descartes after him, envisaged Nature under total male control and his message to the new breed of scientists was "I am leading to you Nature with all her children to bind her to your service and make her your slave." Descartes' statement, "Know that by Nature I do not understand some goddess or some other sort of imaginary power", and that of his contemporary the philosopher Robert Boyle who coined the phrase 'the mechanical philosophy', that Nature should be seen no longer to be "a kind of goddess whose power may be little less than boundless" but as a vast impersonal machine, leave no room for doubt about what these men were up to. Carolyn Merchant says in her recent book 'The Death of Nature'[40] that Bacon frequently described matter in terms of female imagery as a 'common harlot' and that he was well aware of the witch trials then taking place all over Europe. The cruel interrogation and torture of witches became for him a symbol for the interrogation of Nature. The courtroom served as a model for its inquisition and torture through mechanical devices as the tool for the subjugation of disorder and all this was fundamental to the new scientific method of power over Nature. Bacon advocated manipulation of Nature, the technologies of mining and metallurgy and the emerging concept of industrial progress at any price, as well as an even tighter patriarchal structuring of family and state. He fashioned a new ethic sanctioning the exploitation and dissection of living matter (matter = Mater = Mother) and his mentor and protector James I strengthened the misogynist and anti-witch legislation of the time.

The transmutations by the alchemists of old had also been a spiritual quest and had been kept very secret for fear of the ancient knowledge falling into the hands of men who would misuse it. Modern-day scientists have uncovered some of the secrets behind the 'elixir of life' and the transmutation of matter - of heavy metals into radiation - but they work for, and have put this knowledge into the hands of, aggressive and anti-life macho men who are hell bent on the road to total power over Nature, mass destruction and self-deification. The young maiden who is supposedly saved from the clutches of the Dragon in all the legends and sagas about the male solar hero and his exploits is the male-identified, now safely heterosexual virginal woman who no longer knows her Mother (the Dragon who was slain), nor her menstrual, sexual, psychic and creative powers. As a German Nazi said during the preparations for a Holocaust which would be just as horrific as that which had exterminated the witches: "We young men must go out and slay the Dragon so that we can have for ourselves once more the most holy thing in the world - the woman as maid and servant" (echoes of Francis Bacon...). For this Nazi the Dragon meant the Jews. His remark is typical of the way in which all oppressed peoples are treated and described as if

101

they were the despised female, and extraordinary sexual powers and evil deeds are attributed to them/us.

It appears historically as if there has been a clear and deliberate development towards the unlocking of the very powers that the 'sun-god' commands. Such a god resides in the anti-natural, linear, life-negating 'solar' left-hand side of the brain that has been overdeveloped in the patriarchal male at the cost of the Lunar, cyclic and visionary part of the mind.[41] The sun-god in patriarchies is firmly and oppressively male: he is always 'high and dry'. He is never born of the Mother and carries on an obsessive warfare against the Earth and Her magnetic waters and against the Lunar and menstrual powers in women. He cannot tolerate the Lunar rhythms and cycles of Nature, especially those of women. He forgets that sun and fire, in the absence of water and earth create an imbalance that is destructive to life. The ultimate aim of the Witch Hunts and Burning Times over a period of 300 years in Europe was to outlaw Lunar consciousness, to forbid the people to communicate with the Spirits and the Dead, with Nature, with the Moon and the Stars, to make us fear the Night and Her holy Darkness, to either destroy or co-opt the powers of the Wells, Stones and sacred Trees. The Inquisition even tried to pry into women's dreams to eradicate our remaining knowledge of healing and visions. They made us women fear our own strength and psychic healing powers. The witch burnings have been called 'menstrual murders'.[42] From these times - and the last persecutions took place as recently as the early 19th Century in Spain - we have been living in hiding, fearful of being truly powerfully visionary, sexually and creatively female. Some of us are now at last emerging - but oh so slowly - from this excruciatingly painful past...

Nigel Pennick, in his book 'Hitler's Secret Sciences: his Quest for the Hidden Knowledge of the Ancients' (1981), talks of how the so-called 'ley lines' make up a kind of psychic/electromagnetic power-grid across the land and he shows how the Nazi hierarchy were trying to establish these access points in order to des, gain total psychic and physical dominion over the peoples of the earth. For Demeter many centuries before the coming of the Nazis, sacred buildings had been specifically designed by druids, Jesuits, Benedictine monks and other all-male priesthoods to capture and channel these energies for their own exclusive use. To possess these sites was to have control of the 'psychic body' of the country, geomancy being a means to centralise authoritarian power. It is interesting that Pennick points out that the Nazi SS hierarchy was consciously based on a mirror image of the Jesuits, who combined the functions of judges, police and Grand Inquisitors for the church and were the driving force behind the witch hunts in Europe.

In an old medieval romance, 'The Elucidation', we find, says Nigel Pennick, an account entitled 'The Destruction of the Land of Logres'. According to the author of this text at one time there lived at certain Puis (Holy Wells, Springs or Mounds) maidens who would refresh the tired travellers or hunters with food and drink. One had only to go to one of these Puis and state one's wish and food would be brought out of a bowl. One day a king named Amangons raped one of the maidens and stole her bowl. The Puis immediately became deserted and the whole land went to waste. King Arthur's knights took upon themselves the duty of finding these Puis once more and protecting the guardian maidens. They prayed to their god to re-establish the Puis and so re-fertilize the countryside - but to no avail. (No wonder since the patriarchal male god is the supreme enemy of the Goddess, Her sacred Wells and priestesses!)

The land remained fallow, nothing would grow and nothing thrived, for the only way that the Puis could be re-invigorated was to find the Holy Grail, a stone (the Philosopher's Stone of the alchemists, the transformer of power) which could channel celestial energies into the now disrupted system. The Grail is thought to be a holy Stone upon a holy Mountain and is in fact a hidden treasure (the Womb) of the Goddess and is only to be found at fixed cosmic intervals. If the Grail is not recognised then and reactivated, which will not happen as long as patriarchy prevails (as note the rape of the Maidens and the devastation that followed upon this heinous crime against women), at this time, then it will disappear again. And if those without understanding should find it and attempt to use it, it will destroy them. One thinks here of the nuclear physicists. The Puis were the key sites on the system of leys and carriers of subtle energies. Unfortunately Nigel Pennick doesn't seem to have realised that the Maidens were guardians of these places of power precisely because they were the mediums of the Goddess and if they were violated, all of Nature would mourn. Compare this with the stories surrounding Demeter and Persephone, of how all of Nature died when Persephone was abducted and raped by the king of Hades, how nothing grew until she was returned to Her sorrowing and raging Mother Demeter in the Spring.

There have apparently been many UFO sightings near where I live in Pembrokeshire, and Pugh and Holliday write in 'The Dyfed Enigma'

(1979) that they appeared mainly near ley lines and places of electro-magnetic powers. They think that the luminous UFOs and the "mysterious tall beings in silver suits" (who are nearly always assumed to be male although no gender is obvious) might be present day materializations of the 'Fairies' and Nature spirits of old. They write that "The uranium bomb represents the first human device able to produce immediately wholesale global pollution. So deadly indeed is the fallout that long-term effects on people have not yet been fully measured." What these malignant materials do to Nature spirits we do not know. (But we do know that they abominate the chemical fertilisers that are used on the fields and plants.) The horrific effects on humans are there for all to see. The alarm felt by other possible life-forms on our planet is therefore entirely understandable. Thus the mysterious beings prowl around the bomb shelters, scrutinize the air forces and look with distaste on our sewage farms and the chemical clouds fuming from our chimneys. Pugh and Holiday suggest that this is the real reason why UFOs have started to monitor the globe and why they might not be entirely friendly disposed towards human beings either for that matter. We must assist them by cherishing the Earth that gave us life - or She might decide to destroy us all before patriarchal men get the chance to destroy Her, us and all life forms.

Nuclear weapons are, according to Brian Easlea, the ultimate symbol of male 'intelligence' divorced from religious impulse and female cherishing. They are the product of the 'pregnant phallus', the fantasy of the male 'giving birth' without the aid of women. Monstrous weapons of mass destruction are symbolised in terms of a male birth process. The first testing of an atomic bomb by the Los Alamos scientists in New Mexico was called the 'Trinity Project' (father, son and male holy ghost?) and the bomb was talked of as Oppenheimer's 'baby'. The nuclear bombs which devastated Hiroshima and Nagasaki were called 'Little Boy' and 'Fat Man': if they had failed to go off they were to have been called 'Little Girl' and 'Fat Woman'.

Patriarchy is racing to oblivion, attempting to replace all of female-created life with utter sterile barrenness - the 'waste land' of the legends. Male scientists have produced Frankenstein monsters that they cannot themselves control. The splitting of the atom, the first nuclear fission, took place the very year and month that I was born - December 1938. The physicists are trying to extract 'energy' by supreme violation of Nature, robbing Her of Her secrets and treasures. The splitting of the atom is totally anti-natural and produces substances not found in Nature. The biological fission of cell structures produces cells that are akin to the Mother cell and grow organically producing life, but nuclear fission of atoms produces cells that are not like the Mother, that are deadly and radioactive. Male scientists are also attempting to produce male-created 'life' through cloning and artificial 'wombs'. Just what is at work?

The H (hydrogen) bomb was the horrendously destructive end result of masculine 'creativity', the ultimate outcome of masculine oppression of and violence towards the feminine, and it was described appropriately enough by Teller (who was called its 'father') as a 'boy'. If it hadn't worked it would have been a 'girl'. It would appear as if some men are trying to undo the whole of natural evolution and are wanting to 'thrust' us back to the chaos before creation: it is almost as if they want to transform the earth into a nuclear furnace like the sun, to make it resemble their archaic male godhead. It was no accident that the Nazis chose the solar swastika as their symbol. The sun without water becomes deadly...

Brian Easlea talks of scientists who are looking forward to and planning for a future when man (sic) will have outgrown the childish pursuits of "sensing, love-making, dancing and singing" and will become truly "mechanical, electrical man" - i.e. definitely not Lunar, watery, magnetic, vibrating and resonating with Nature/She – when 'he' will become 'pure mind' encased within metallic cybernetic bodies that are 'immortal' and never die, and will also never live in any sense of the word known to Nature or intended by the ever-living, ever-dying Lunar Mother.

But there are, thankfully, on the positive side physicists like Fritjof Capra who have come full circle and realise that everything in the Cosmos partakes of the eternal dance of the Goddess. Some scientists are now talking of the ecosphere - the world as Gaia, the living, breathing, creating and conscious Earth Mother.

COMING FULL CIRCLE

It was no coincidence that my last and most important and far-reaching pilgrimage in search of Her holy places should have its beginnings in the Women for Life on Earth march to Brawdy, near where I live in Wales, at the beginning of June 1982. The Welsh county of Dyfed is harbouring at Brawdy the biggest American underwater spybase in the world. Its radar system can detect Russian nuclear submarines anywhere in the world. It is also built for a 'first strike' which makes the whole of Dyfed a target if there should be a nuclear war between the superpowers. Women had marched from Cardiff to Brawdy and from Aberystwyth, in North Wales, and joined up on the 6th of June in front of the US base. I had joined the Aberystwyth march as it came through Fishguard and walked with it for the last two days before it reached its destination.

The year before Ann Pettitt, living near Carmarthen in south-west Wales, had conceived of the idea of getting together a group of women and children to march all the way from Cardiff to the US base at Greenham Common, near Newbury in England. She and her women friends had felt that men had always left their homes and families to go to war and now was the time for women to leave their homes and menfolk and march for peace - to show our outrage at what the ruling men of all nations are planning for our Mother the Earth and for all coming generations. They knew that Greenham was the base where preparations were being made to install the dreaded American-controlled Cruise missiles at the end of 1983 and knew that if these weapons were ever deployed it would mean the beginning of the end. Because their protest had been virtually ignored by the media the peace women decided to chain themselves to the railings of the vast perimeter fence surrounding the base in true Suffragette fashion. Some of them then set up a Women's Peace Camp at the main entrance to the base - and there it has remained to this day (March 16th 1984), in spite of all the hardships - the constant harassment from police, soldiers and vigilantes, the evictions, arrests, court appearances and jail sentences, and the incessant noise from the helicopters and planes flying overhead - and the traffic on the main road - the heavy glare of the searchlights during the long winter nights, as well as the rain, hail, snow and mud which the women have had to suffer.

The extraordinary thing is that Greenham Common is very close to Avebury/Silbury and it is almost as if the ancient Mother is inspiring and transforming the women there, helping them to rediscover and use age-old women's magic. Their actions have also inspired women all over the world and similar camps and protests are mushrooming in many countries. A rumour is currently circulating that Greenham was a place of execution of Wicca in the 17th Century.

From the demonstration at Brawdy I travelled to London to meet up with my Swedish anarcha-feminist friend Pia Laskar, who was coming to join me in the pilgrimage which was to extend from Avebury/Silbury to Callanish in the Outer Hebrides and was to last for one month. Pia and I had spent some time together on Crete at Easter of the same year. We were going to hitch lifts all the way and stay with friends of mine up and down the country.

We first went to stay with Hilary Llewelyn of 'Wood and Water' magazine who then lived at Swindon. Next day we went with her to Avebury, Silbury and West Kennet long barrow. We walked amongst Her ancient Stones at Avebury, and again experienced the darkness of Her tomb. The three of us lay holding hands in a circle on top of Her Belly/Mound. This time I felt myself as a new-born child resting on my Mother's pregnant belly. It felt bittersweet, joyous and sad all at the same time. I have all my life carried with me such a sadness and anger about my own beautiful and creative mother's life, her pain and sense of failure at not having been able to succeed as an artist, her poverty, loneliness and premature death.

In the evening when returning to Swindon we got a lift with a man who turned out to be the worst kind of fascist 'born-again' christian businessman. He had specifically picked us up so as to lecture us about the dangerous Pagan influence of Avebury. The patriarchal god and his lackeys forever lurk near Her sacred places, trying to contain Her and us - but to no avail.

We had decided to travel to Glastonbury in south-west Somerset, and on the way we passed by and stopped off at Stonehenge where some 'freaks' were beginning to gather with tipis, tents, caravans and wagons in a field near the monument. Every year at the Midsummer Solstice the traditional and 'new age' 'druids' come here to do their rituals and thousands of them gather for a month-long music festival. Stonehenge is aligned to the Midsummer Solstice sunrise and in the early dawn when the rituals are performed the 'druids' are let into the monument enclosure. The whole event is very male-dominated, but some of the powerful women who live in the mixed tipi village in the valley amongst the Black Mountains near Carmarthen - an astonishingly beautiful and wild place - play a relatively active part. There are many men about who want to pose as 'new age' gurus though. Stonehenge is usually shut off to the public and one can no longer walk among the stones, only encircle them from outside the perimeter fence.

Pia, who had never been there before, felt especially after having experienced the maternal presence and living body of the Mother at Avebury/Silbury, that there are overpowering, oppressive and negative energies dwelling in and around these stones as if the place had patriarchal vibrations. Perhaps some particularly gruesome sacrifices were once carried out there. I had always felt that the enormous stones at Stonehenge are somehow not within the landscape, as are those at Avebury and other sacred places, but are unrelated to it and tower above it, creating disharmony. As we saw before the blue stones brought from Goddess temples on the Preseli Mountains are Lunar in character. But the final building and 'erecting' of the sarsen stones with their trilithons was done by the Bronze Age 'Beaker people' who it seems already had a male priesthood and chieftains. Early relatively simple and organic centres of psychic power became by the time of the completion of Stonehenge (around 1600 b.c.) both unwieldy and too complex, and possibly also uncontrollable. It appears that signs have been found of a possible disaster happening at Stonehenge and other similar sites. It is possible that the male priesthood tried to 'overload' and 'overwork', to amplify and concentrate the energies to such an extent that a 'fuse' blew. Molten stones have been found which indicates extreme temperatures and the existence of these is totally inexplicable except by such a blowout. Anyway, whatever the reason it seems that the Druids abandoned the stone circles and withdrew into their oak groves for purposes of worship and magic workings.

It is interesting to note that the aged woman-oracle at Delphi, who was originally the oracular priestess of Gaia and Her Python, was driven literally 'mad' by the incessant demands upon Her from the male Apollonian priesthood. The name Delphi derives from an ancient Greek word meaning 'womb'. It was said by Roman writers that this same Apollo was worshipped at Stonehenge by the Druids. Apollo was, however, not originally a sun god, but a god of ecstasy, inspiration, oracles, healing, poetry and music (he played the lute), as well as of shamans. But this was in Asia, before he was imported into Greece. Originally Shamanesses were particularly important in Asia (in parts of Siberia there were societies right up to the time of the Russian revolution in which the Shamanesses outnumbered the shamans and were credited with great powers), and it seems to me that Apollo and his all-male priesthood of homosexuals had taken on exactly the functions of the great Goddess Brigid of the Celtic and Pre-Celtic peoples. Apollo's sister was, by the way, Artemis/Diana, Goddess of the Moon and the Witches, who was worshipped even into medieval times in Europe. It is striking how popular Stonehenge is among present-day male-dominated occult, 'druidic' and 'new age' groups. It is also a very popular tourist attraction, complete with coachloads of visiting city-dwellers and the inevitable hot-dog, fish n' chips and ice-cream stalls which do a roaring trade throughout the summer months. Thankfully this is not the case at Avebury or at Glastonbury Tor. Unlike the so-called 'civilised' people of today the ancients lived in harmony with Nature and practised their magic rituals collectively and openly. With the emergence of patriarchy, with its violence and warfare, the Druids kept the ancient knowledge coded in secret numbers, letters and runes, and in sacred geometry.

We left Stonehenge and arrived the same day in Glastonbury in the pouring rain and went to stay with Janet McCrickard for the night. She has done much work to recover knowledge about the Sun Goddess and about Brigid. Glastonbury, too, draws to it many 'mystics' - feminists, 'new age' people, devout christians, Goddess women. It is felt to be a very ancient and holy place with its indwelling female spirit still very much alive.

We again explored the Tor and went to Chalice Well, also called 'Blood Well', to drink of its rust-tinted (iron content) and blood-like waters. I have now read Geoffrey Ashe's recently published book 'Avalonian Quest' (1983) in which he suggests that the extremely ancient 'old Church', rumoured to have been built by Joseph of Arimathea in 63 a.d., was dedicated to 'Mary, our Holy Mother', possibly at a time when the Marian cult within the catholic church didn't yet exist.

It was the Council of Ephesus in 431 a.d. which first authorised the title 'Mother of God'. The church, which no longer exists, is so old that there are no records of precisely when it was built. The reason it was dedicated to Mother Mary is that Glastonbury was already an ancient sanctuary of the Goddess. The hills, including the Tor, make the outlines and form of a gigantic Woman Goddess figure, as at Avebury/Silbury. This region was very important long before the Celts came here and excavations in the moors have revealed the remains of what are said to be the oldest roads in the world, some dating back as far as 3200 b.c. The Tor was said by the Celts to be the home of Gwyn ap Nudd, king of the Fairy folk and lord of Annwn, the Celtic subterranean Otherworld. He was the leader of the hunt and king of the Dead, and an important figure in Welsh mythology.

Geoffrey Ashe thinks that Ma or Matrona was worshipped on or in the Tor, the same Goddess in triple Lunar aspect that I came across in Cologne, and was said to be the Guardian of Wells and the Giver of all Life. Her name was changed to Madron, which simply means 'Mother'. At a later stage She became fused with the Celtic Goddess Morrigan and was named Morgen. Morgen lived on the 'Isle of Apples' (Avalon) which was ruled by nine sisters. She was their chief, a healer and enchantress who flew through the air and could change shape. She welcomed the wounded king Arthur to Her island and promised to cure him. In the Arthurian romances of medieval times She becomes Morgan le Fay, but whereas the Celtic christians could accept Her magic as benign, the medieval christians saw Her less and less as a healing enchantress and more and more as a malignant witch. Her island community of nine shamanesses (a Lunar number) and Her magical powers recall other such communities that existed in Celtic times. Still in the first century a.d. there was a group of nine 'virgin' priestesses on the Ile de Sein, off the coast of Brittany. They cured the sick, could take animal shape, foretell the future and control the weather.

The ancients probably danced the labyrinth to the top of the Tor in procession and then entered into it to enact a very special ritual within Her womb, inside the Tor itself. It was said that within the Tor was the Cauldron of Cerridwen, and perhaps the ritual procession through the Tor maze was the 'search for the Grail' (Cauldron) of rebirth, wisdom and immortality. One remembers how the Pentre Ifan cromlech in Wales was also called 'The Womb of Cerridwen' and how the Cauldron of Cerridwen is also her 'womb' within which magical transformations take place through the use of water and fire. If the Tor is the vagina of the Goddess - as clearly seen from aerial photographs - then Chalice Well is Her menstrual flow. Apparently no such red-tinted water is to be found outside of this area and must come from an unknown source very far away. It is possible that within the secret subterranean chamber inside the Tor there was kept an actual iron cauldron in which was prepared a hallucinogenic liquid from the water of the Well which was taken by the initiates to help them perceive another reality - but this is only a guess. I would assume that women first designed and made iron cauldrons as Brigid was a Goddess of smithcraft. It must have appeared miraculous to them how it was possible by generating great heat under the cauldron (clay pots could not be fired in this way: iron has a very high melting point) - to change herbs and foods from their natural forms into completely different substances. Herbs and mushrooms that are poisonous in their natural state can in this way be changed into healing, hypnotic and trance-inducing medicines and drugs, and it was women who knew how to bring this about. I remember hearing stories as a child of ugly old 'witches'/hags who were stirring their cauldrons in caves or dark huts and putting into them 'disgusting' things like frogs' legs, fly agaric mushrooms and so on. Now we know, of course, that 'Amanita muscaria', a fungus that grows abundantly in Sweden, if used properly prepared and carefully, is highly hallucinogenic and was used by the ancients in their religious rituals to induce states of ecstasy. The patriarchal Vikings also used such fungi when going into battle to induce berserk rages which helped them to overcome their fear of death. The 'old hags' knew very well what they were doing: they were the healers and midwives to the common people as we now know. It is interesting to note that in the English language there are expressions like 'a veritable fountainhead of knowledge/wisdom', 'all is well' and 'to feel well'. There are rumours of an actual well or spring within the Tor itself.

Seven miles from Glastonbury on the land of Pilton Farm and with the Tor in full view there have been held over the last ten years or so many fairs and festivals drawing vast crowds of both 'freaks' and 'politicos'. Recently there have been CND festivals, Green Gatherings and a women-only summer camp. I took part in the five-day long Green Gathering of 1982 which was an attempt at pulling together CND-supporters, Eco People, Feminists, Gays, Pagans, Animal Liberationists and so on - something like 'The Greens' in Germany. There were differences of opinion and arguments concerning women-led and women-only actions at Greenham Common during which there were powerful clashes between men in CND and women from the Greenham camp and from Women For Life on Earth. The gathering took place over the ancient festival of Lammas (August 1st). On Lammas Eve some Pagans (members

111

of Craft covens) organised and led a public celebration within a consecrated circle. Some sixty people, including two of my sons took part, and the Craft members felt that this was the firstly open and publicly celebrated manifestation of the old Religion that had been held in Britain for several hundred years. The same night I held a meeting in the women's marquee about Womanspirituality and showed the slides of my paintings.

Next day, in the glorious sunshine, a large crowd of people danced and spiralled ecstatically for hours to the tune of 'King of the Fairies', accompanied by drums and pipes. Towards dusk the same evening we had a women-only Goddess ritual within a circle led by women from the Dianic Grove group of the Matriarchy Network. During the whole of the Green Gathering we had our own space in and around the women-only marquee where we held workshops of various kinds. The fact that there was a women-only space caused a lot of bad feeling among some men and some male-identified women, and the fact that there would be a women's camp after the Gathering in the same fields caused a lot of hostility. But in spite of all sorts of threats the women's camp went well and about 400 women came to it. It all took place within the presence of the Tor and the Goddess.

On the road from Glastonbury to Bristol there is the city of Wells, presumably named after its waters. In the cloister walk of the fine Wells cathedral there is carved a Sheela-na-gig in the roof. Here the monks meditated and walked around and around an enclosed garden. I wonder what they thought if and when they saw Her? A few miles from Wells there are the Cheddar Caves that stretch for miles and there is Wookey Hole which is a very ancient sacred cave indeed and was the home, according to legend, of the Witch who demanded human sacrifice. Wookey Hole descends through many different layers, through a labyrinth of underground lakes and rivers and caverns. It is truly magnificent. Celts lived for a long time in these caverns and the fourth cave is a former burial chamber. Together with the River Axe the caves were once a source of inspiration and worship for the Celts who lived on the slopes of the Mendip Hills. It seems as if awesome sounds are heard within the caves caused by the waters, the alternately trapped and escaping River Axe and the inrush of air. "The dreadful cavern spake: She many a sigh from her full stomach cast which issued thro' her breast in many a boist'rous blast," wrote Clement of Alexandra in 189 a.d. "In Britain is a certain cave at the side of a mountain, and at the entrance a

112

gap; when, then, the wind blows into the cave and is drawn on into the bosom of the interior, a sound is heard as of the clashing of numerous cymbals." Presumably this was an oracular cave with its in-living priestess, who interpreted the sounds, music and rumblings of the cavern as being the voice of the subterranean Mother. The story goes that an 'evil witch' (inevitably) lived here demanding sacrifices and that a christian monk came here from the community at Glastonbury and when confronted by the old woman threw 'holy water' at her, upon which she turned into a stone. Today when one visits Wookey Hole the guide points out a large, dark, strange-looking and humanlike stone within the first cavern and says that this is the 'petrified witch'. Perhaps this particular stone, in fact, had some strange powers and had worship centred around it as the 'guardian deity of the Underworld' and was used in oracular work. Strangely enough he also called some stalactites high up in the roof of a cave 'Joan of Arc'. Archeologists have found a hammered out socket under the 'witch's' left breast and in the floor below the decomposed remains of a wooden stake.

The waters of the River Axe have been used by a mill since the 17th century to make the finest hand-made papers - which are still being made today. The river emerges from the Mendip rocks. The mill is on the walk that tourists make through the caves.

After having visited Avebury/Silbury, Stonehenge and Glastonbury Tor within the space of just three days Pia and I felt that we needed to recover and we spent a few days in Bristol doing 'ordinary' things like seeing friends and relatives and going to pubs. In Bristol itself there is an area called Hotwells where long ago there were hot and healing springs. There are no signs of them now unfortunately, but in Bath, going from Bristol towards Avebury, the hot wells and springs were used for healing purposes until very recently. The Romans built the baths from which the town takes its name, in which the water is naturally warm, and dedicated them to the Goddess Sul. The place was a great Roman healing centre - Aquae Sulis - and was, like all sacred wells, springs and healing water places, under the protection of the threefold Mother Goddess. The waters of Bath cured rheumatism and skin diseases in particular. The Roman baths can still be visited. In the 18th century the fashionable upper classes used to come to Bath with its healing mineral springs to 'take the waters'. It has just occurred to me that the police station in Bristol is called (of all things) 'Bridewell'! In so many places it is only the place names that indicate the ancient sanctity and presence of the wells, springs and fountains. The waters are long neglected and covered over by concrete and asphalt, by roads and buildings - much to our own peril and loss of natural sources of healing and power.

We next set off on a very long trek towards the north-west of Scotland by easy stages. We stopped off in Birmingham to talk and stay the night with Anne Berg who exhibits with me in the 'Woman-Magic' exhibition. To stand, hitchhiking under the 'Spaghetti Junction' in Birmingham - where motorways from all over Britain join and criss-cross each other - is perhaps one of the most horrific things one can think of doing. This is the ugliness of patriarchy in extreme - its dirt, dust, noise, pollution and foul air in which nothing organic can thrive.

We also stayed one night in Livingston, a new town outside of Glasgow. A friend of mine has lived there for many years slowly going crazy because of the soullessness and apathy of the place, where huge housing estates in which every block is completely the same as every other and where everything is placed according to straight lines, and grids dominate the landscape. The whole 'new town' is completely inimical to organic growth in any form of shape.

Leaving Livingston, standing near the motorway in the rain, we felt pretty miserable. But we were lucky and got a lift with a male 'freak' who was driving a very long distance in the direction we wanted to go. In fact, in the end, he went out of his way to take us to our destination, a little boat jetty in Dundonnell, by Garve in Ross-shire. We had been invited to come and celebrate the Midsummer Solstice with some women from the Matriarchy Network at the home of Cathy Dagg. She lives on an isolated peninsula near Ullapool where the ferries go over to the Hebrides. We were, however, ultimately aiming to be at Callanish on the Isle of Lewis, to go to the stone circle there for the Solstice. We were to meet up with some 'Earth Magic' artists there on that day.

Cathy lives in Scoraig, across the water from the jetty where we were standing, in an alternative community of about 50 people who live around the peninsula in small cottages and houses. It is a mixed community and is enlightened enough to produce its own electricity from windmills, but not radical enough to treat an independent and creative Goddess-feminist like Cathy with respect. We had found that there is no road to Scoraig, only a winding path that would have taken us five or six hours to walk with our heavy rucksacks. The only other way to reach her home was by getting a lift across the water by motor boat.

Shamanka at Callanish (1982)

Cathy had given me a phone number to call to ask for a boat to come over and fetch us, but when I called, it was quite late and I found that the owner of the boat was in the middle of a drunken party and no way wished to go out on the choppy water to fetch some unknown females. He told us to sleep as best we could in an empty van standing on the jetty and that "perhaps" someone would fetch us next day! We had visions of being stuck here for the next few days without being able to reach either Cathy or Callanish. In the meantime we went on a search for a cup of tea and somewhere to warm ourselves. We had to knock on the doors of the few houses there were (no such things as cafés in this remote place), and were welcomed in by two elderly women who turned out to be Gaelic speaking sisters. We sat by the peat fire drinking tea and eating scones while the two old women graciously told us about themselves. We discovered that they had both been born in this cottage, had never married, and would die here. We felt happy and comfortable and returned early next morning for yet another cup of tea after sleeping rough in the back of the van all night.

The mountains of the north-west of Scotland were the abode of the Goddess Cailleach and were the land of the Picts whose domain extended from the northern isles of Shetland to the small isles of the

115

Inner Hebrides, eastwards to Loch Lochy and south to the sources of the Forth. The Picts were a pre-Celtic people and thus very ancient, and it is possible that the word 'pixie', meaning 'fairy', referred to them. They were also rumoured to live in mounds, underground halls and chambers and to possess great magic powers. It seems that their art, carved on stones, is very different from Celtic art, and is unrelated to any other contemporary pictorial form. They tattooed themselves all over with images of animals and plants and went into battle in the nude, women and men together. They were greatly feared by the Romans.

The Gaelic-speaking Celts or Scots came over from Ireland originally and colonised Pictish land from the early centuries of the christian era and in 844 a.d. they gained political power in the country. The Vikings or 'Norsemen' (sic) occupied the Hebrides, the Shetland Islands, the Orkneys and the coastal areas of the mainland between the 9th and 13th centuries a.d. The early christian missionary St. Columba came over from Ireland and created a religious community on Iona in 563 a.d. From there missionaries went to the mainland and founded other cells and christian communities. It would seem that St. Columba was still a bit of a Druid and had magic skills. Iona is an enchanted island with a very ancient feel about it.

Recent excavations on the Shetland Islands and on the Orkneys have uncovered Neolithic dwellings that can only be called 'Goddess houses'. The dwellings are contained within thick outer walls, which are egg-shaped, and Her body is described by the chambers inside. The entrance corresponds to the vulva. The best known Goddess, as temple and habitation, is at Skara Brae on the Orkneys. These are reminiscent of the Goddess temples on Malta and at New Grange. Three-dimensional underground mazes called 'weems' were also built by the Picts. The word 'weem' is similar to 'wamba' (cave) and 'wame' (womb). Underground chambers called Fogous or Souterrains are often found within enclosures in ancient villages in the western part of Britain and especially in Ireland. The Celtic Scots have in recent times been oppressed and colonised by the English and the Gaelic language and culture have been deliberately destroyed. As in Wales the Celtic language in Scotland was not allowed to be spoken and 'culprits' were punished harshly. But in Wales/Cymru there has been a great revival of the native language as well as music, poetry and culture in general, which doesn't seem to have happened on the same scale at all in Scotland. We were told that the young people do not care for Gaelic, nor for the culture, up here in the Highlands and islands.

The following morning we were woken up by a very wet Cathy knocking on the door of the van. She had only just found out now, in the morning, where we were, and had in a fury rowed across the water in a leaking rowing boat. The man who is in charge of the one and only motor boat wouldn't let her use it as he didn't think she'd be able to handle it being a mere woman. Later in the day we were all ferried across.

For the next few days we rested while waiting for more women to arrive and went for long walks over the wild mountains. We found crystal clear lochs (lakes) in the valleys, saw a flock of wild deer fleeing from us, rested on rocks by the sea in the sun and even saw an eagle or two. It was astonishingly beautiful. One day we saw the forlorn figure of a woman standing on the jetty. It was Lyn Stag of the Matriarchy Network who had come all the way from London. She was also the only woman, besides us, to turn up after all. Since like this it wouldn't be much of a Summer Solstice celebration, Cathy and Lyn decided to come with me and Pia to Callanish instead to join up with my friends there.

On the gloriously sunny morning of June 20th we set off, carrying heavy rucksacks containing tents, to walk the winding mountain coastal path that would take us to where we could get a boat across to Ullapool. We walked all day and when it got dark we put up our tents by the side of the road that we had by now reached. In spite of it being hot and the bags heavy we felt light-hearted, happy and even exhilarated by the fresh air, the sea, the smells of blossoms and herbs and the beautiful landscape. We felt a bit like mountain goats, sturdy, bouncy and obstinate. In fact I have seldom felt so well and healthy and fit as during the month-long journey that year. Very early in the morning we got up and packed the tents, then had a quick dip and wash in a loch before making the final walk, now downhill, to the little boat that takes post across to the mainland. We arrived in good time both to do some shopping for provisions and to take the morning ferry across to Stornaway on the Isle of Lewis.

We arrived at Callanish stone circle, one hour's bus ride from Stornaway, at 1.30 p.m. on June 21st, the Midsummer Solstice. We found my friends camped nearby in a field where they had already been for a couple of weeks. They had slept within the stone circle overnight to await the Solstice sunrise. Among the Earth-Magic artists we met up with there was John Sharkey, who I have known for many years, Lynne Wood from Australia (now taking part in our 'Woman-Magic' exhibition instead of Marika Tell), and Jill Smith (Bruce). Both Lynne and Jill are performance artists and shamanesses. I found that they had arrived at Callanish by much the same route that Pia and I had taken. They had also made their own spiral journeys to the centre, visiting many sacred places and circles along the path.

In some Goddess-way Jill, Lynne and I are linked together through St Non's Well. To all three of us the wells of Brigid/Bride are unfolding some of their magic and wisdom and we are as a result being deeply changed. It was with Lynne that I went on a Full Moon night before St Brigid's day to St Non's Well, while at the same time Jill was at Bride's Well on the Isle of Lewis. They had before this both been together at Glastonbury to do some Goddess/women's work with a group of women at the Tor and the Chalice Well, and from there Lynne had come to me to be at St Non's Well at Full Moon, while Jill travelled to the Hebrides. Psychic links between Chalice Well, St Non's Well and Bride's Well were established through us. May She live and come yet again into Her true being.

John Sharkey, who wrote 'Celtic Mysteries' some years ago is now finishing off a book he has been writing about the Dragon-shaped Hebrides (He-Bride-s) and the Neolithic Goddess culture on these islands. May he be successful in this, and give Her due respect and reverence.

There are three stone circles at Callanish, all within view of each other. The two older, and smaller, stone circles were built to align with the moonrises and settings above a sacred mountain called The Silver Maiden and The Sleeping Beauty, thirty miles away. The largest and perhaps most recent stone circle - and the one that we had specifically come to spend time at - is laid out in the form of a Celtic cross and is most extraordinary. It stretches its 'arms' down to the water on two sides and has been likened to a 'cathedral' because of its eerie beauty, dignity and size. Its stones are the most gracious and deliberately shaped, like silvery slender flames growing from the ground, that I have yet come across in a stone circle. The strange thing is that no photographs or slides taken of the stones convey what they are actually like. According to local lore they cannot be counted. The Vikings when they came here called them the 'Trolls' and they appear as tall hooded figures turned to stone during a processional walk. In the centre of the circle - or cross - stands a 15 foot high stone, appearing like a swirling, dancing shamaness as it seems to move and glow. An ancient legend tells that people arrived here by boat from the sea, anchored in the bay and danced through the stone avenue to the circle led by a shaman/ess with a blackened face and bird's wings. We do not know what rituals they performed. There have never been attempts to destroy these stones, as happened at Avebury during the witch hunts. They were merely half-submerged in peat, which had to be cleared away in order to reveal them. Although the islanders became Calvinists, which is the worst, most puritanical and bigoted form of christianity, I expect that they still had a sneaking respect for and a sense of the ancient sanctity of the stones - a sense that it would be 'unlucky' to harm them.

It is difficult to put into words the experience of being here on this barren island where no trees grow. Here there is only peat, sea, rocks, and the stone circles. We are so close to the elements and have a feeling of being 'at the beginning of time', totally primordial. Never have I experienced the Sun as being so close and so overwhelming, never have I experienced such sunrises and sundowns as here. And on these islands this might be the only week in the whole year when it isn't raining and stormy. The Sun went down around eleven o'clock at night, leaving a reddish-orange glow over the horizon for hours: around three o'clock in the 'morning' (I would call this night-time) it appeared again above the sea. There was just nothing between us and the sun but the sea and the stones. It was stupendous and wonderful, fearful and joyous. This experience of the sun will stay with me forever. The only industry on the island appears to be peat-digging, which leaves strange formations in the landscape where it had been dug and mounds of peat drying everywhere in the sun. There is a wonderful smell from burning peat fires, rich and aromatic.

That first night - the night of the Midsummer Solstice - we all stood amongst the Stones to watch the sun go down. It felt very powerful and holy. Later, around midnight, in the dark of the Moon, the four of us women (Pia, Cathy, Lyn and myself) went back up to the large stone circle. We sat down in the hollow area, which had once been a grave, in front of the tall swirling central stone. We held hands in a circle, while we ourselves were encircled by the stones, and slowly began to hum together. What then happened felt extraordinary to all of us: we became as if possessed by the 'Banshee', the Wailing Goddess. We started to wail

119

and scream and howl. It felt as if the sound came from within the Earth itself, from within our bellies... It felt extremely ancient...as if we had tapped into the veritable Dark Mother within our collective selves. I have never before felt such a sound coming out of myself and such deep dark emotion. Afterwards we all thanked each other...danced our way out of the circle and made our way back to the camp-fire feeling transformed and strangely bonded together.

We heard later that a few self-styled male 'druids' who were present had been worrying and thinking that we would be up to some 'evil witches' magic' there in the circle! They seem to be still at work co-opting and controlling, trying to take over women's knowledge. The next day, much to our sadness and regret, Cathy and Lyn had to return home. After they had left in the morning we got involved in hurried preparations for going on a day-long trip to the 'Sleeping Beauty', the sacred mountain thirty miles away. This mountain was here long before the Stones and is one of the most ancient in the world. Inevitably the British government had sought permission to dump their abominable nuclear waste in this very sacred peak, but they had, fortunately, been refused permission to do so. The outline of the 'Sleeping Beauty' against the sky is that of a vast recumbent woman. One can clearly make out Her head and profile, then Her neck and two breasts, Her womb and legs. The likeness is quite uncanny and extends over and includes a number of mountain ridges.

As I said before the earlier and more ancient stone circles were built to align with the Moon's risings and settings over Her head, breasts and womb. She, the Mountain Mother, was there first of all. We started off on our journey to Her by car: this time there were six of us - four women and two men - to the oldest stones. By this circle there is the remains of what was once Her holy well. It has been deliberately neglected and has become murky and overgrown. I felt myself strong enough and felt called upon to start uncovering it, and within a few minutes we were digging out large chunks of grass, earth and slimy weeds to find the stone structure of the Well underneath. Lynne had felt wary of doing this, because one never knows what energies one might suddenly be letting loose after centuries of imprisonment and blockage. She herself had had the experience of ritually uncovering a holy Well that had been forgotten and found disused under a house in a small town in Wales, only to find that the now released energies were too sudden and too powerful and turned malignant for the women present. The women who lived in the house above the Well all developed some form of trouble or illness to do with the womb and Lynne got accused of being a 'black witch'. Not surprisingly she was wary. I knew about this but felt that it was the right thing to do, to release Her well. While I was digging a mare in the field came and stood with her head above mine cradling me. When we left after a while to carry on with our journey I began to feel distinctly weird as I was sitting in the car. I was beginning to feel 'crazy' or as if I was going off on a 'trip'. I felt afraid. This lasted for perhaps an hour during which a glass fell inexplicably out of my spectacles, but luckily they didn't break. As we came nearer to 'The Sleeping Beauty' my attention was diverted and I felt more relaxed and less afraid.

We started a climb that was going to take us a full four hours, up higher and higher ridges and down the slopes in between. It was exhausting and the higher we climbed the harder the wind blew. It was difficult at times to keep our balance up there. Finally we arrived at the summit - as high as we could get - on Her womb/belly. Here the ancients had built a cairn of stones piled up on top of one another into a cone shape. I had thought that once I reached this cairn I wouldn't move again as I was so tired. I sat resting. Then I saw to my amazement and wonder the vast sweep, as of a processional path here high above the world, towards the two breasts, both of which have cairns as nipples placed on them. It occurred to me that the ancients must have somehow come all this way up and then danced towards Her breasts and head. This felt a bit like Glastonbury Tor with the same sense of natural shapes changed as if to distort perspectives and space and time, to transport one into an 'Otherworld' of timelessness. This must have been a cosmic mountain, the world navel where all realities merge, the belly button from which all of creation was born. Here I was in the presence of a primordial and more ancient Mother than I had ever known before. I felt ecstatic, experienced a sudden surge of energy and went striding off towards Her breasts along the sacred Path that I could sense, only to find that the distances were so much vaster than I had imagined. I walked for a very long time. Here was also the sensation as at Glastonbury Tor of walking along the vast back of a huge animal. Here She was Dragon, Sphinx and Lion all in one. From a distance She had been a sleeping woman, but from up here She appeared as a recumbent Lion. She is like the Moon; Virgin, Mother and Hag; Tomb Mother, Mountain Mother and Animal Mother; She who shines for all, She who shape-shifts, She who transforms Herself...

I know that I howled and cried and shouted with Her up here beneath the sky and in the wind. The experience of having been at one with the Cailleach the night before within the stone circle in the dark of the Moon was still strong within me. By now we had all dispersed in different directions, all of us preoccupied with our own inner journey. I arrived by Her vast neck, the ridge leading to Her head, but something in me wouldn't let me go any further. I couldn't walk upon my Mother's face: it felt blasphemous. Others went striding past without a care. I tried again, but came up against the same internal barrier, Pia had by now reached me and told me that she had felt the same resistance to walking on our Mother's face as I was experiencing. So there we stayed in awe and wonder and thankfulness...in joy and sorrow...with tears and laughter. It was indescribable...

It felt as if it had been destined that we were to come here, Pia and me...memories of our experience together on Crete feeling 'taken' by the Mountain Mothers, of not wanting to leave Her/them. We climbed back down Her many ridges and arrived back at the road after what felt like weeks, exhausted and dazed. We waited for the others to arrive and after a brief visit to a pub to warm ourselves we drove back to the camp. Then, the day after, we also had to leave. We travelled on the road passing the 'Silver Maiden' and saw from yet another angle how dignified and majestic She is. We were on our way to taking the ferry over to the Isle of Skye, which is very beautiful, green and lush. We put up our tent near Portree at night in a field by a stream with the blue snow-capped mountains in the distance. It was lovely and peaceful, and also wild. In the morning we travelled to the ferry which sails over to the mainland, going back by a different route from the one we had taken on the way there. We travelled back through the breathtaking landscape of the Highlands with its high mountains and deep, clear lochs and forests towards Glasgow where we yet again stopped off for the night with my friends in Livingstone.

We were now heading for Sheffield where there is quite a large Matriarchy group. It was the women of this group who had brought 'Woman-Magic' to the north of England and had organised its tour up there. The exhibition has been shown from January 21st to February 2nd (Candlemas/Bride's Day) 1979 in Sheffield. Anne Berg and I had been there both to hang the exhibition in January and to take it down at Candlemas, and while we were there we had been taken by one of the women, Helen Ives, onto the moorland around Sheffield where we had visited the very magical Barbrook stone circle. These Stones are small and are placed near a river in the moorland landscape that feels very invigorating and positive to me. The three of us had stood in a silent triangle, arms upstretched and humming together. Every one of my visits to this stone circle has felt very good and joyous to me. At a Matriarchy Network gathering of about 35 women from all over the country in Sheffield over the Spring Equinox in 1981 we all went to this circle and danced around the stones in a long chain in the pouring rain. It felt exhilarating. I had come here from the funeral of a dear friend and lover, so this visit felt particularly healing and supportive. Helen had also taken part in the treading of the Maze at Glastonbury Tor on Beltane Night 1980 and had witnessed the miraculous lightning storm that night.

Pia and I now made our way to Helen's house in Sheffield. We found that by yet another 'coincidence' the very next day - Saturday, June 26th - was the sacred day of the annual 'well blessings' in the small towns and villages around this part of Derbyshire. On the Saturday we set off in Helen's car to visit once again Barbrook Stones on the moors, then Arbor Low Stone Circle. The extraordinary thing is that all the enormous stones at Arbor Low lie flat on the ground and it isn't clear whether the ancients meant them to be like this or whether they were later desecrated. Helen said that she had always experienced grief when coming here. She feels as if something terrible has happened in this place. It certainly has nothing of the high and positive energies of the Barbrook Stones and it is very probable that the different stone circles and sacred places up and down these islands and in Brittany were charged with different and complementary energies. The Earth Spirit travelled between them and energised them at different seasons of the year; different rituals were enacted at every place. Together they celebrated the mystery of the different stages in the monthly and yearly birth, life, death and rebirth cycles of the Goddess at the sites where She was experienced alternately as a young Girl, a menstruating, sexually mature, birth-giving Mother, and as an old healer/midwife/hag, The Tomb Mother, reborn again as the young and delicate crescent Moon.

The same day as visiting Barbrook and Arbor Low we also took part in the processional well blessings in Youlgreave and Bakewell. It seems that the well dressings originated in Tissington, which is nearby, and it is said that the reason for this lovely custom is that during the Black Death in 1348-49, when hundreds of people died in the villages all around, Tissington kept free from the contagion, "this being attributed to the purity of its Wells; the people, says one tradition, from that time dressed them annually in thankfulness." A second tradition has it that in 1615 when there was a great drought and all the land was parched and dry the Wells in Tissington still gave water freely. The well dressings consist of large floral images on a clay and wood backing set above each Well. Seventy people are needed to make five such images and it is painstaking and slow work to set thousands of flower petals, leaves, grass, hair and moss into the wet clay. Only natural organic things coming from the Earth can be used and it is mainly women and girls who spend months designing and making the intricate images, which mostly have biblical motifs, but often exhibit Pagan symbolism too. On June 26th all the images are in their place over the Wells, although some Wells are no longer visible and many are disused. After mass in the church the whole congregation, led by a priest or vicar and containing a choir, wander from Well to Well, saying prayers over them and blessing them. The incredibly radiant and colourful images live only for a week and then die. Many tourists come nowadays to these villages to see 'the blessings'. In the official 'Well Dressing Guide' it says: "Wells - particularly 'miracle' and curative wells - in many places in Britain and abroad are decked with flowers and greenery on ceremonial occasions, but nowhere in the identical Derbyshire way. The custom can only have developed from the age-old fear and worship of water-gods and spirits. Into rivers, springs and wells people of all countries the world over have at times cast virgins (patriarchal myths of Virgins sacrificed to Her Dragon dwelling in the Well?), children, choice animals, and fruits and blossoms as thanks-offerings for the gift of water, or as bribes against drought and floods. The ancient Britons had some such custom; certainly the invading Romans had, and St. Ann's Well, Buxton, may have been wrongly named by men (sic) who in the 16th century found on the well bottom a much defaced fragment of a statue which they thought to be Saint Ann (Mother of Mary) but was probably of the 'nymph' Arnemeza or Aquae Arnemetia, Roman Goddess of Wells. When the Pagans ceased making their live sacrifices, Christians expressed thankfulness for water by holding services by springs and wells, and decorating them with flowers. But exactly how the Derbyshire picture flowering was initiated may never be known."

Pia and I were now coming to the last day of our month-long journey together and decided to close this particular circle on the spiral by visiting the Women's Peace Camp at Greenham Common, coming full circle from the Women For Life On Earth march to Brawdy at the beginning of June. We stayed with the Greenham women for one night in a caravan by the main gate, took part in their discussions and felt thoroughly enthused by the magic and power of what they have undertaken to do. As I see it they/we are daughters of the Goddess who were sent here to stop the truly obscene spectacle of huge phallic missiles being hauled around the countryside on vast hideous juggernaut lorries - and all this in the presence of our Mother at Silbury/Avebury.

On the 12th and 13th of December 1982 I returned to Greenham, travelling by coach with some women from Fishguard, to take part in the enormous 30,000 strong women's exorcism of the US base. Women encircled the entire barbed-wire perimeter fence, holding hands, planting live candles all around it, spinning woollen spiders' webs over the seven gates, placing images and clothing of beloved children on the fence, weaving a woman-and-life-vibrating embrace around this ugly and repulsive monstrosity. I will never forget the beauty and mystery of the candles burning all along the fence in the twilight, which created images like one finds at an ancient shrine...with women singing, moaning, keening and humming all around...On the next day, December 13th, which marks the festival in Sweden of the Queen of Light, Lucia, we placed our bodies in front of the gates, trying to prevent vehicles and personnel from either entering or leaving the base. We got flung in the mud and dragged off again and again as vehicles forced their way through us inch by inch. All the while the women kept singing 'You Can't Kill the Spirit'. It felt very strange in the evening of that day hitching back by the old road to Bristol and passing Silbury Mound as it loomed out of the shadows and the gathering dusk.

Since this Greenham visit many more magical and astonishing events have been enacted by the Peace Women. I also took part in the 'Women Reclaim the Earth' conference in London organised by the Women for Life on Earth Network in October 1983.

Here my ever-unfolding Spiral Journey must for the moment come to an end. Knowing that the future is extremely uncertain, and in spite of the fact that cruise missiles are now installed at Greenham Common and elsewhere in Europe, the struggle, courage and sacrifices, particularly of women, continue to give me hope. I put my trust in the Goddess and bid you farewell for now.

YOU CAN'T KILL THE SPIRIT
SHE IS LIKE A MOUNTAIN
OLD AND STRONG
SHE GOES ON AND ON AND ON...

Blessed Be,
Monica Sjöö,
March 1984

NOTES

1. My article'The Goddess at Avebury' was published in the American journal Womanspirit (2000 King Mountain Trail, Wolf Creek, Oregon 97497-9799, USA) in 1978. This shorter prose-poem which I called 'Life, Death and Rebirth at Avebury - February 19 78' was published separately in the same journal. It is also included in the journals Women Are the Real Left/wider We: Towards An Anarchist Politics (England, 1979) by Keith Motherson and myself, Politics of Matriarchy (1979) and the Swedish anthology of women's writings Kvinnor och Skapande (Women and Creativity) published in 1983.

2. Both of these important books were published by Thames & Hudson, London. Michael Dames calls himself a 'matriarchal man' in a letter to me. He has had a similar experience to mine, one of overwhelming grief and sorrow, in the presence of Silbury Mound, and wrote his books because of personal conviction and belief rather than because of academic considerations. He is, like me, an artist, as well as a historian. His books have been ridiculed by the male academic community.

3. Sibylle van Cles-Reden, The Realm of the Great Goddess, in which she traces the megalith builders all over Europe. Published by Thames & Hudson, London, 1961.

4. Thom wrote Megalithic Lunar Observatories in 1967.

5. Martin Brennan, Boyne Valley Vision, London, 1980. His book is illustrated with his own beautiful drawings throughout.

6. Read the wonderful book by Marija Gimbutas, The Goddesses and Gods of old Europe 7000-3500 B.C., Thames & Hudson, London, 1968, concerning neolithic imagery and symbolism.

7. Katherine Briggs, A Dictionary of Fairies, Penguin, London, 1977.

8. Janet McCrickard's article 'Great Mother Sun', published in Woman spirit, Fall Equinox issue, 1982.

9. Robert Graves, The White Goddess, Taber & Faber, London, 1961 (first published 1948).

10. Quoted from the Matriarchy Network Newsletter, Winter 1982. This issue was edited by Cathy Dugg in Seoraig. north-west Scotland.

11. I describe similar sacred Goddess mountains on Crete in my article 'A Pilgrimage to Crete', which was published in the Spring Equinox issue of Woman spirit; it was also included in Arachne, journal of the London Matriarchy Network, 1983.

12. John Michell has written a series of books about Earth Magic and Ley Lines including The View Over Atlantis (1969), The Flying Saucer Vision (1972), City of Revelation (1972), The Old Stones at Land's End (1975) and The Earth Spirit: Its Ways, Shrines and Mysteries (1975) (part of the Thames & Hudson 'Art and Imagination' series, ed. by Jill Purce). His books are a wealth of interesting and exciting information and ideas, but they are unfortunately tainted with a sexist and patriarchal bias.

13.Robert Graves' The White Goddess was the first book I read, now 21 years ago, that first told me of the Goddess and of Matriarchal cultures and thereby opened up to me a whole area of knowledge and visions. His work gave me hope - and this was years before the beginnings of the present Women's Movement - and inspired my painting and reading.

14. I took this information from the article 'Goddess Power in Ancient Ireland' by Bridgit Morgan in the Politics of Matriarchy journal, 1979. The journal was, together with the booklet Menstrual Taboos, published by the former London Matriarchy Study Group that I was a member of and contributed writings to.

15. I have used much information about the People of the Sidhe/Fairy Folk from the very interesting book The Fairy Faith in Celtic Countries by W. Y. Evans Wentz (1911). He was an American who at the beginning of the century travelled in all of the Celtic countries when the ancient oral/story-telling tradition was still alive and well. He wrote down the tales and legends which were recited to him as he sat around the peat fires in the cottages of the peasants. Margaret Murray's books The Witch Cult in Western Europe (1921) and The God of the Witches (1931) are important and early sources of information on the Wicca and the old Religion, as well as on the Fairy Folk and the wise women as healers and midwives to the people.

16. Concerning the Culdee church read 'Interview with a Modern Witch' in Margot Adler's book Drawing Down the Moon, Beacon Press, Boston 1979.

17. Gerald Gardner, The Meaning of Witchcraft, Aquarian Press, 1959. The author writes from the perspective of being both an anthropologist

and an intiated witch (he also founded many covens) about the history of Britain and Ireland. It was only in the 1950s when the last remaining laws against witchcraft and spiritualism were repealed that he was able to publish his books.

18. Jørgen Andersen, *The Witch on the Wall - Medieval Erotic Sculpture in the British Isles*, George Allen & Unwin, London, 1977. Academically written by a Dane, but worth getting because of its many astonishing images of the Sheela-na-Gig and information on where they are to be found all over Britain.

19. I have told the story of my paintings and especially of the "Woman-Magic' exhibition and the painting 'God Giving Birth' in the article 'Art is a Revolutionary Act' which was published in Woman spirit in 1980.

20. Jean Markale, Women of the Celts, 1975. The author is a Breton and teaches Celtic art and history at the Sorbonne University in Paris.

21. For an imaginative account of the Druids and of the Celtic 'love of ambiguity', poetry and the fantastic, read John Sharkey's *Celtic Mysteries: The Ancient Religion (1975)* in the Thames & Hudson 'Art and Imagination' series. John is himself a poet with an Irish background.

22. Guy Underwood, *Patterns of the Past*, Abacus Press, 1972. The author was a dowser who still at the age of eighty walked the ancient trackways and dowsed the stones and sacred sites. He found that iron interferes with the subtle currents and underground waters of the Earth Spirit.

23. Read Sibylle can Cles Reden's book (mentioned in note 5) about the Maltese temples and Neolithic temples and tombs generally in Europe.

24. The Ancient Religion of the Great Cosmic Mother of All by Monica Sjoo and Barbara Mor, Rainbow Press, Trondheim, Norway, 1980. Information on the 'Burning Times', the old Religion and so on is contained within.

25. Janet McCrickard has written on Brigid/Brighde in Priestess, a small journal that she edits from Glastonbury. The first issue was at Imbolc 1983.

26. Gertrude Levy wrote The Gate of Horn: A Study of the Religious Conceptions of the Stone Age and their Influence upon European Thought in 1946 (Faber & Faber, London). This is one of the many scholarly and important books by women that have been virtually

ignored and forgotten but are now being rescued by the Women's Movement. The author talks of the ancient caves as the sanctuaries/wombs of the Goddess, and of the neolithic Cow Goddess in particular, as being also the gateway and enclosure of the herds.

27. Francis Hitching, Earth Magic, 1976. Again a very interesting work, but patriarchal.

28. My article 'Treading the Maze at Glastonbury Tor, May Eve 1980' was originally published in Woman spirit and in Wood and Water in 1981.

29. Geoffrey Ashe has written a number of books, among them The Virgin in which he explores the worship of Mary (Mariology) of the Catholics and traces it back to the ancient religion of the Goddess. His most recent book is Avalonian Quest (1983). In 1980 he wrote a pamphlet called The Glastonbury Tor Maze. He has also done a lot of research on the Arthurian legends and lives at Chalice Orchard at the foot of Glastonbury Tor in a house that was formerly owned by Dion Fortune, known for her books on the occult.

30. For a discussion of the Right/Left brain hemispheres read Moon Moon by Anne Kent Rush (USA, 1976).

31. Gertrude Levy, op.cit.

32. For an explanation of ancient women's Mysteries of Transformation read The Ancient Religion of the Great Cosmic Mother of All, op. cit.

33. Article by Hilary Llewelyn in Wood and Water, Samhain issue 1982, about wells in Brittany. Wood and Water is the small journal of a mixed group of Goddess- and eco-centred pro-feminists and radical Pagans of which I am a contributor and member.

34. Sibylle van Cles Reden writes of well shrines in Sardinia, op. cit.

35. Anne Kent Rush, op. cit., writes of the Black Mother in Moon Moon,

36. The important books by Starhawk are The Spiral Dance: A Rebirth of the Ancient Religion of the Great Goddess, Harper & Row, New York, 1979, and Dreaming the Dark: Magic, Sex and Politics, Beacon Press, Boston, 1982. Starhawk is a Feminist Wicca who is involved in the anti-nuclear struggle in America.

37. Most of the information for this section I have taken from Danmarks Helligkilder (Denmark's Holy Wells) written in 1926 by August F.

Schmidt. Concerning the Goddesses in Norse mythology read Merlin Stone's Ancient Mirrors of Womanhood, Vol. II, New Sibylline Books, USA, 1979. P. V. Glob, The Bog People, Faber & Faber, London, 1969, writes of the Iron Age people who made sacrifices to the bogs and to the Goddess in Denmark some 2000 years ago.

38. Brian Easlea has written the excellent *Witchcraft, Magic and the New Philosophy, Science and Sexual Oppression: Patriarchy's Confrontation with Woman and Nature* (Weidenfeld & Nicholson, London, 1981) and *Fathering the Unthinkable: Masculinity, Scientists and the Nuclear Arms Race*, Pluto Press, London, 1983.

39. Read Witches, Midwives and Nurses: A History of Women Healers, a pamphlet by Barbara Ehrenreich and Deirdre English, New York, 1974.

40. Carolyn Merchant, The Death of Nature: Women, Ecology and the Scientific Revolution (New York, Harper & Row, 1980). She expresses similar ideas to those of Brian Easlea. For a different approach and perspective read the feminist writer Susan Griffin's Woman and Nature: the Roaring Inside Her, New York, Harper & Row, 1978.

41. Lewis Mumford, The Myth of the Machine: Technics and Human Development, London, Secker & Warburg, 1967, and The Pentagon of Power, London, Secker & Warburg, 1971.

42. Penelope Shuttle and Peter Redgrove, *The Wise Wound: Menstruation and Everywoman*, London, Gollancz, 1978. This is an astonishing book which explores the menstrual Lunar powers and mysteries of women.

WOMEN'S DREAM-JOURNEYING ACROSS SALISBURY PLAIN:
RECLAIMING EARTH OUR MOTHER FROM THE MILITARY

30 April-4th May 1985

A call had gone out from the Greenham women, for women all across
Britain to gather at Avebury to attempt a walk across the firing ranges of
Salisbury Plain. So I & Jill & her baby Taliesin (born naturally in the
Tipis near Llandeilo in Wales) hitched from Pembrokeshire on 29th
April because we wanted some time at Avebury & Silbury to ground
ourselves in the sacred place before the action began. Both Jill & I are
artists & have been deeply moved by the Goddess in Her manifestations
on Wiltshire Plain where every hill, mound , stone circle & long barrow
form part of Her living body on a gigantic scale. The Avebury
monuments form the concentrated visual sculpted images of the Goddess
within the centre of Her larger & more ancient body.

Only two other women had arrived; women from Galloway who I had
learnt to love & respect during the Ten days at Greenham in September.
That night the four of us slept under the sky on Silbury, unthinkable to
put up tents here...one doesn't put pegs in one's Mother's belly. As a
result we had a cold & windy might during which at one point both Jill
& I experienced as if we were watched over by a Fairy presence.

In the early morning the four of us went to greet Swallowhead, the
vaginal opening in the white chalk embankment which is the source of
the sacred river Kennet, which originally meant "cunt". There we
meditated & then we went across the field to the nearby West Kennet
Longbarrow.

There was time for breakfast in the friendly Ridgeway Café & then to go
to Avebury village to meet up with some friends who were arriving. We
joined a group of punk-women from Greenham who were sitting in a
circle within the Stones. Police were also gathering by now &, when later
we were sitting at the foot of Silbury having our lunch, we were
approached by them & warned not to entertain any ideas of camping for

the night anywhere in the vicinity. I don't think, however, that anyone ever had any doubts concerning where we would all sleep that night & by the late afternoon we simply all went up on the mound & there we stayed put. After that we were never bothered by the police. What could they have done after all?

The night to the 1st of May is Beltane & we were here to celebrate the Goddess even though Silbury, as I've already explained, is a Lammas mound & the Harvest Mother. It would not have been possible for us to celebrate Beltane within the Stone circle because of the bigotry & fear of the people who live in the village itself.

We made a Beltane Fire & then gathered for a ritual & to discuss what we wanted to do. By now Starhawk, who is an American feminist Wicce/Witch & is the author of "The Spiral-Dance" & "Dreaming the Dark", had arrived. I had been telling the women of how I had been waiting now many years for women to gather here so as to give our healing & love to the sorrowing Mother. Starhawk suggested that we cast a circle, ground ourselves & dance a Spiral-dance... & so we drummed & danced & chanted in great joy on the mound/womb. I talked of how the ancient Neolithic peoples experienced, without any distinction between Self & the World, the earth as a Maternal being & that everything was alive & partaking in the sacred. The ancients lived the agricultural year as the unfolding of the life of the Goddess from Maiden to Crone, the temples here were Her seasonal reality & the people moved with Her from place to place with the changing seasons of the farming year. The Avebury monuments are aligned within the "pubic" triangle of two rivers meeting. The rivers were seen to be the superhuman blood streams of the Goddess gushing from Her Earth womb. The ancients believed that life began in the waters & rivers, streams, wells & springs that are sacred to Her.

Finally we all slept curled up close together on Her belly & all around. The following morning we packed up, had breakfast & then we set off walking along the Ridgeway, ambling through the lush & green Wiltshire countryside, passing through innumerable villages, and picnicked in a churchyard. It was a very long day & we finally arrived exhausted to set up camp in the rubbish-dump on Redhorn Hill on the northern edge of Salisbury Plain in view of the barbed-wire fences of the M.O.D. land. The hollows of the dump (not much rubbish here in fact) were quickly transformed into a comfortable women's space: tents, fires, cooking & women's talking & singing all around in the dusk.

In the morning of the 2nd of May we (we were a hundred women or so) gathered around a fire to discuss what to do next, since Red flags, signifying firing in progress inside the ranges, were up. We did a grounding & singing meditation to centre ourselves & then the decision was taken to simply walk through the fences and barricades of police, because this was what we had come here to do. We had come to reclaim the sacred Salisbury Plain from the military & we were not going to be stopped.

In the meantime some women were sitting along the fences facing the military & the police all the while chanting "Earth is our Mother, we must take care of Her - we walk upon this sacred ground with every step we take". I had joined them for a short while but was overwhelmed by tears & grief at the sight of these strong & beautiful women & then in contrast the patriarchal waste land, of destruction & barrenness facing us on the other side of the barbed wire fences.

To me, as to the women there, our spirituality & our love of the Mother is in no way to be seen apart from the political struggle against patriarchal oppression in all its forms...repressive abortion laws, institutionalised poverty for women worldwide & male violence, pornography & rape, clitorectomy & mass starvation in Africa, dowry, murders in India, uranium-mining on Aboriginal lands in Australia & USA, nuclear testing in the Pacific & Cruise Missiles in Europe...

Before walking onto the Larkhill firing ranges three of us decided to do a little ritual burying a tiny Goddess/woman clay image in the central fire-pit left from the meeting. Grete, a potter from Cornwall, had brought a number of such images to be buried throughout our journey; dreaming the land.

When we had finished our ritual & went up to the fence to join the other women we found no-one there & were told that all the women had been rounded up & arrested! This was a moment of terror & panic...for a split second I felt as if we were the only three women left on Earth & on us rested the responsibility to save the planet. Then ... we simply charged ahead & to our relief we saw the women further up circling & circling, dancing & singing while surrounded by police who tried to contain them. We joined them. We argued with the police who finally understood that either they would have to arrest every one of us or they would have to let us go through. After a while orders came that firing would cease for the day & that we could carry on our walk.

Some women had been arrested but were let out at night.

We felt that we would have to keep closely together & to walk at a slow pace because a number of women on the walk were carrying babies, & there were older women & women with blisters on their feet. We didn't want to be divided, to be picked off in small groups by the police. No way was it possible to stray off the ugly track-road used by tanks & military-vehicles since live shells, missiles & mines were embedded in the land all around us. There were no animals in sight, no bird song & hardly any trees to give shade from the hot sunshine.

It was eerie & dreary walking here & hard going indeed.

That night we slept & put up camp by the Bustard Hotel, still on military land which I hadn't realized until we were again faced with a large number of police next morning. They were yet again attempting to barricade our way & this happened again & again this day, on our last lap to reach Stonehenge by the afternoon. The police seemed to be playing a "cat & mouse" game with us...except that we refused to be the mice. A number of times we were faced by lines of army vehicles & police vans...women being dragged off as we walked many abreast, arms linked, & being encircled by other women trying to free them.

Every time at the last minute, before anyone actually was arrested, orders came through to let us go. We heard police-men (& women) cussing & swearing & throwing their helmets on the ground in a temper at this. At last we left military land behind us & celebrated by dancing & drumming & singing & picnicking on the now safe grass.

This was Friday - day of Freya the Great Goddess of the North where I come from in Sweden. We saw animals again in the fields, but were struck dumb with anger & pain when we stopped on the road near a herd of cows that looked maltreated & ill-used. Some of the cows could barely walk because of the size of their udders & some of them had such bad legs that they were dragging themselves along painfully bit by bit. To us this was yet again a painful & ghastly reminder of the fate of mothers - whether animal or human - in Patriarchy & it was all too much.

The Goddess in Her manifestations at Greenham Common (1984)

We had an argument with the arrogant farmer who had a slick answer to everything & to whom profit is clearly the only thing that matters. Some women were in tears.

We had been warned that we would not be able to camp near Stone Henge, but now a message came through that we could use the auxiliary car park, situated right next to the toilets, the tea caravans & the official tourist entrance to the Stones. So...there we put up camp, stared at by tourists arriving in their coaches who read with astonishment the signs we put up saying "Salisbury Women's Peace Camp" & texts explaining what we were doing here & why.

By now we felt utterly powerful, a magically invincible army of women/witches who could overcome just any obstacle put in our way. Some women cut holes in the razor wire-fences surrounding Stone Henge & slept within the Stones that night.

I had felt uneasy & had said so about heading for Stone Henge because I feel this is a place of heavy & negative male energies that cannot be reclaimed by women. We now had many discussions & disagreements

136

concerning the energies here & about the history of the Stones. The outer larger Sarsen stones forming the Trilithon circle were erected relatively late in time by the already patriarchal & hierarchical warlike Beaker people in the Bronze Age. They were probably already introducing a male Solar cult to these isles to replace belief in the ancient Sun Goddess Grainne/Ainu. It is not unlikely that they used slave labour in "erecting " these stones & possibly even human sacrifice at their foundation. The slaves would have been precisely the darker & smaller Neolithic Goddess people who had so lovingly created Silbury & Avebury. Heavy & brooding energies are felt by these stones who appear megalomaniac in their hugeness & uniform size & they appear to hover above the Earth rather than belonging organically with her, as do the stones at Avebury. It also seems no coincidence that Stone Henge has been so cherished by patriarchs throughout the ages & is so even now, as witness the Druids, the New Age male gurus & the male freaks of the "sex, dope & Rock & Roll" squad.

On the other hand the inner shoe, or Cauldron, shaped Blue Stone circle is Lunar & was called "The Womb of Cerridwen" by the Wicce. These stones are more ancient & were brought from the Preselau Mountains near where I live in Wales/Cymru. Everyone asks always 'how they were brought to Stone Henge' but never "why". Considering that they more than likely originally were part of an ancient stone circle of Cerridwen in the sacred mountains one may well ask "why".

The so-called "Aubrey holes" (now filled with ugly concrete), together with the "Heal Stone", are the oldest part of Stone Henge & their purpose is to measure & predict Lunar Eclipses.

Saturday 4th of May was the Full Moon total Lunar Eclipse & therefore this was perhaps the place after all for raising powerful female energies at this time. Great numbers of Stone circles & Standing Stones have as their most important function the prediction of Lunar Eclipses which makes me think that this must have been THE time of the highest psychic/sexual female energies of the Goddess & the ancient women. We simply no longer know.

The sacred sites are the acupuncture points of the Earth's body where powerful underground water currents spiral & electro-magnetic energies emerge through cracks in the Earth's crust to inter-react with the large amount of quartz in the Stones & with energies radiating from Cosmos from the stars, Moon & Sun. They can in fact be called the sensitive centres of Earth's central nervous system. The Ancients knew this & they cherished Her & tuned into Her telepathically. But...with emerging Patriarchy the ruling male hierarchies have also known of these vital psychic energy centres & have attempted to control & manipulate them. In Medieval Times the Church & the monasteries were built on these places. In Germany the Nazis dabbled in the Occult & studied the Ley Lines. Presently Nuclear Missile bases like Greenham are placed in the vicinity of Silbury & Stone Henge, uranium is mined precisely from under Aboriginal Dream lands in Australia & ancestral burial sites of the Natural Peoples in USA, ancient sacred islands in the Pacific are pulverised through testing of Nuclear bombs...& so it goes on.

The ancient women & men loved the Earth - the indigenous peoples still speak of their love of Earth the Mother - & they heightened Her beauty & fertility & their own psychic awareness & powers through work with Her within the sacred Stones. Many Stone circles in Cornwall - the Nine Maidens, the Merry Maidens - are associated in legend with women singing & dancing thereby presumably activating the Stones & themselves into ecstatic trance-states & great, to us unknown, powers. Patriarchal men on the other hand want to control these sacred places for the sake of death, power-over & utter destruction.

The Greenham women felt that Stone Henge, imprisoned by razor wire fences & looking distinctly like Greenham itself, must be liberated & reclaimed for the people. The punk women also told Starhawk in no uncertain terms that they didn't want any structured or led ritual when inside of the Stones. They then went on & did a funny, in spite of themselves, inspired "Bog roll ritual" which really took off swinging & moving & piss-taking.

On the morning of the 4th of May I woke up with my hand red & swollen which seemed strange considering that I hadn't been aware or any bite of an insect the night before. The following day pus came out of my hand & it healed fast with the help of the women's loving care & the innumerable rescue-remedies & homeopathic salves that they carried with them. Rumour went about that perhaps I had been bitten by a serpent! Or perhaps shot at with a Elf-dart...who knows. Strange times.

In the morning of the Saturday a few of us had gone down to the river Avon to fetch water to take to the Stones because we feel that they badly need the Water-element. We also had water from Chalice/Blood Well on Glastonbury Tor & other Holy Wells. While we were sitting by the

138

river - a couple of women swimming in the cold water - a great &
beautiful swan came towards us on the river. One of the women had just
been asking for a sign that we were doing the right thing here at Stone
Henge & this seemed indeed to be a positive answer.

At 6 o'clock p.m. we cut holes in the fences & snaked our way into the
Stones across the field all the while singing "Return to the Mother" while
tourists & police looked sheepishly on. We were now about 150 women
since many women had come from cities like London & Bristol for the
weekend. In there we gave much loving care & energies to the Blue
Stones & we danced amongst them, chanted, meditated, lit candles &
dreamed ecstatically for hours. The sky had been clouded over most of
the afternoon & evening but around 9.00 p.m. the sky cleared, a hush
went about, & we could clearly see the eclipsed Moon. We stood then,
entranced in the grass outside of the Stones facing Her & hummed &
sang softly for a long time while a delicate sliver of the Lunar crescent
first showed Herself & until she was again fully visible in Her glorious
silver radiant roundness. This was true magic indeed.

Many women slept that night amongst the Stones in the Moonlight. In
the night there were hustles with the police & the women had to leave
the Stones. Women were also arrested when a smaller number attempted
to set up camp for the next few days at Beethes Farm after the majority of
the other women had left because of the sudden bad weather.

During the whole of the walk Zohl - an Australian woman who has lived
two years at Greenham & whose calling it is to bring the message to us
from the indigenous dark peoples of Australia & the Pacific of the
destruction of their lands & peoples at the hands of the British, French
& US nuclear & military interests - carried with her a Black Aboriginal
"Talking Stick" which she held high in the centre of our circling &
winding Spiral-dances to send healing & strength to those peoples in
their struggle for survival.

We felt during this Walk reclaiming this land that we were connecting
with the Aboriginal peoples who still follow the Rainbow Serpent as She
journeys through the sacred lands. We were Dreaming our lands as they
do theirs. It is a chilling thought that Uranium when it is mined is
Rainbow-coloured & that both amongst the Hopis or USA as well as
amongst the Aborigines of Australia there are the warning prophesies
that if uranium is mined (the veins of the Mother torn out, the Rainbow
Serpent disturbed in Her Dreaming) from under their sacred lands, the

resting places of the tribal Dead ones, it will lead to utter destruction. These peoples as were the wise women/Wicce in Europe until the end of the Witchhunts/Burning Times are still the guardians of our Mother, the Earth & their warnings must be heeded before it is all too late.

I felt that by giving our Woman energies & love to the Blue Stones within Stone Henge we will have changed the energies in there forever.

The energies from this week & the immense sense of empowerment for a long while stayed with every woman who was on this Walk & we felt Blessed.

19/6/85 Monica Sjöö Dark Moon Wales | Cymru

Resource-list:

Michael Dames "Silbury Treasure -The Great Goddess Rediscovered" (1976) "Avebury Cycle" (1977) by Thames & Hudson

Monica Sjoo & Barbara Mor : "The Ancient Religion of the Cosmic Mother of All" (Rainbow Press, Trondheim, Norway 1981) To be soon published in USA by Harper & Row ,translated to German & published by Labyrinth in Braunschweig West Germany in march 1985

Monica Sjoo "The Goddess/es of the North" (Article written for & published in Arachne, the London Matriarchy journal, 1985 c/o A Woman's Place - Victoria Embankment- Hungerford House-London WC2

Janet McCrickard pamphlets on Brighde/Bride & on the Sun Goddess

Adam McLean writings on the Lunar Fire Quarterday Festivals

Starhawk "Dreaming the Dark -Magic , Sex & Politics "1982. Beacon Press

John Michell "The Earth Spirit: Its Ways, Shrines and Mysteries " (1975 Thames & Hudson "Art & Imagination'" series)

Carolyn Merchant "The Death of Nature Women, Ecology & the Scientific Revolution" (Harper & Row, 1980)

Penelope Shuttle & Peter Redgrove "The Wise Wound: Menstruation and Everywoman" London, Gollancz ,1978).

Diane Bell: Daughters of the Dreaming George Allen & Unwin, 1983

Brian Easlea "Witchcraft, Magic and the New Philosophy", "Science & Sexual Oppression: Patriarchy's confrontation with Woman & Nature (Widenfeld & Nicholson, 1981) "Fathering the Unthinkable : Masculinity , Scientists & the Nuclear Arms Race" (Pluto Press 1983)

Susan Griffin "Woman and Nature: the Roaring Inside Her" (Harper & Row, 1978) & "Pornography & Silence (Women's Press, 1981)

Anne Cameron "Daughters of Copper Woman" (Press Gang, Canada 1981)